A Simplified Life

Verena Schiller is an Anglican religious sister of the Community of the Holy Name who for the last 25 years has lived as a hermit in North Wales.

p. 28
p. 45
p. 175

p.28
p.45
p.115

A Simplified Life

*A contemporary hermit's experience of
solitude and silence*

Verena Schiller

CANTERBURY
PRESS
Norwich

First published in 2010 by the Canterbury Press Norwich
Editorial office
13–17 Long Lane,
London, EC1A 9PN, UK

Canterbury Press is an imprint of Hymns Ancient and Modern Ltd
(a registered charity)
St Mary's Works, St Mary's Plain,
Norwich, NR3 3BH, UK

www.scm-canterburypress.co.uk

British Library Cataloguing in Publication data

A catalogue record for this book is available
from the British Library

978 1 84825 025 3

Originated by The Manila Typesetting Company
Printed and bound in Great Britain by
CPI Antony Rowe, Chippenham SN14 6LH

Contents

Acknowledgements

I owe enormous thanks to many people for their encouragement, wisdom and support. Without each and all of them neither my life as a hermit nor this book would ever have been possible.

To Ani, my mother

Foreword

Many people might feel they have little in common with a solitary nun living a life of silence on a remote peninsula in Wales. But Sister Verena speaks to that part 'in each one of us, a solitary centre and silent place that longs for attention and space'. Just as the natural landscape of the Llŷn Peninsula became her mentor, so too she shows us how the contrasting noise and crowds of urban living, or unchosen simplicity of lifestyles, can teach us.

Hers is not a romantic account, nor blurring of the exacting external conditions of the day to day, nor of the conflicts of internal struggles. Surrounded by beauty, yet Sister Verena negotiates the loneliness and doubts, anxiety, weariness and despair that make it hard to pray or even just to sit in silence and think. All of which speaks to our universal human experience ... for if a nun can acknowledge such things, so we too may look to our own doubts and fears.

Sitting in Sister Verena's small cabin, looking out over the holy island of Bardsey, I am reminded of the rich heritage of this land and of all our world. The poet R. S. Thomas also lived in the area, and explored the natural world of Pen Llŷn and its history in his relationship with God, writing:

> These very seas
> are baptised. The parish
> has a saint's name time cannot
> unfrock.
> (*The Moon in Lleyn*)

Sister Verena too sees the detail of nature, the intimacy of landscape and the presence of history. She comes to rely on the 'givenness of the present moment' in life, and names this as of God as she learns to watch, wait and listen on behalf of us all. For though it is often when one is not looking that God reveals himself, that entails being open and alert. In showing us how we too might learn this, she helps us on our own personal pilgrimage and gives us cause for hope.

Archbishop of Wales

Prologue

On the tip of the Llŷn Peninsula, (see Map1 p. 18), that north-west finger of Wales bordering Cardigan Bay, stands a small cabin tucked into the corner of a field. A window frames an island, the holy island of Bardsey, a sheer rock rising out of the sea some 4 km or so across the Bardsey Sound that separates the island from the mainland. Enlli is the island's Welsh name meaning Island of Currents, so called because of the treacherous cross currents of the Sound and coastal waters which secure the island's fastness. It is a rock that can be seen from almost any vantage point on Pen Llŷn along the coast or inland. On a clear day from the peak of the is-land, Enlli Mountain, the whole of Wales lies mapped out from coast to coast and from mountain range to mountain range: from Snowdonia down the ridge of the Cambrian Mountains to Strum-ble Head and beyond. Yet the island itself has its back turned to the mainland, a cliff drop of some 167 metres enhancing the sense of mystery that often surrounds small islands. Enlli does not give up its secrets easily. The sheer cliff face of Enlli Mountain hides the gentler slopes to the south and west and the two arms of land that reach out towards the setting sun. On clear days Ireland and the Wicklow Hills break that western horizon. This is Enlli, the 'Island of the 20,000 Saints', where over the centuries dating back to the early Celtic Church, small numbers of hermits and monks have made their home and many others have come on pilgrimage in search of their 'place of resurrection'. Some of these allegedly laid their bones there: the legendary '20,000 saints'. There are traces of pre-Christian life on the island too but almost certainly it became a place of Christian prayer from as early as the late fifth or early sixth centuries.

Today a traveller or pilgrim in northwest Wales finds their inner eye drawn down this long finger of land that forms the Llŷn Peninsula, drawn to Bardsey and the wide unbroken horizon beyond. Island and mainland are as one: those headlands and coastlands, the sparsely populated hamlets and villages with their pilgrim churches set along the ancient pilgrim routes. According to expert geological research Bardsey was never joined to the Llŷn Peninsula but to mid-Wales at least 70 km down the coast. Yet without doubt island and mainland stand as one in a unity of a different quality from that of geographical separation by the waters of the Sound or the geology of millennia ago.

Above the cabin's same window that frames the island of Enlli is a poster of another holy island: Skellig Michael, or Sceilig Mhichil in Irish, another island some 217 metres high, lying off the west coast of the Ring of Kerry in southwest Ireland, (see Map 4 p. 157). It is a rock – *Sceilig* being the Irish word for rock – that can be seen for miles around, from as far south as Bantry Bay to the Dingle Peninsula and far beyond to the Blasket Islands to the north. To our ancestors it would have beckoned irresistibly, this rock on the western horizon, the seeming edge of the world, nothing beyond it except the unbroken waters of the Atlantic Ocean. Each evening it disappeared into the setting sun. For them this horizon was the rim of a flat world circled by the sun, a three-tiered universe of heaven, earth and underworld. The island's peak would have seemed nearer heaven than anywhere else that they knew. This island too drew pre-Christian seekers and later early Celtic monks and hermits. As on Enlli off the west coast of northwest Wales, these men risked their lives in search of their 'place of resurrection', and were known to have made their home there certainly from as early as the sixth century. A cluster of six beehive huts, two oratories and a graveyard with a striking rough-hewn cross are huddled together on a narrow plateau near the summit of the island above cliffs that drop sheer on every side to the rocks and churning sea below. This monastic lavra[1] points to a life of unbelievable austerity lived under conditions so extreme that it is almost impossible to imagine, let alone to reconstruct, in the very different culture of our present age. Was there something here comparable to the Syrian and Egyptian deserts to which the first known Christian hermits withdrew as early as the fourth century? Here on Skellig Michael a similar quest may have drawn these first intrepid seekers after God to a life they also saw as an authentic following of the gospel precept: 'Go sell all that you have . . . and follow me' (Matt. 19.21). This was a life of few escape routes, a life that encouraged a human journey of singleness of heart and spirit, mind and body interpreted by them in ways so different from those of our twenty-first century in the West. The ocean was their desert; the rocks and headlands their mountains; the unremitting elements, sparseness and solitude their sense of place and space and threshold. On Skellig Michael the elements rage, the winds and storms whip the rocks clean, the sea and spray guard the island's remoteness and inaccessibility through all but a few weeks in the summer months. This island and adjacent mainland are more rugged than Bardsey and the Llŷn Peninsula but both would seem to beckon as the desert had beckoned those early Christians of Egypt and Syria.

What drew those first Christian monks and hermits in the fifth and sixth centuries to these western seaboards of Celtic Britain and Ireland? What continued and still continues to draw pilgrims, monks and hermits, and seekers from many walks of life, to these same coasts and holy islands? What has been the experience of a contemporary hermit now, at the turn of the twentieth/twenty-first centuries?

---

1 Lavra: a small monastic community of prayer and silence with some degree of communal life normally centred on the Eucharist and the Divine Office.

For over 25 years there has been a hermit in this small cabin on Pen Llŷn, looking out day and night over headland and Sound to Bardsey; visiting the island most years for short periods but never drawn to live there; once making a pilgrimage to Ireland from Glendalough, the site of St Kevin's 'monastic city' in the Wicklow Hills and then across Ireland to the far west coast and the Ring of Kerry to Skellig Michael itself (see Map 3 p. 146).

The thrust of what follows is neither an academic nor a historical or literary work as such. Rather it is a following through, a weaving together of three journeys, three stories: the story of a place, a personal journey lived out within that place, and the universal journey shared by all men and women – our human condition.

This then is a book about these three journeys and in particular the journey of one person's life – my life – lived here in solitude and silence as a hermit nun. For most of us a journey involves travelling from place to place or country to country, for our work, for a holiday, or for whatever other reason takes us away from home. We enjoy exploring new landscapes or the culture of another land and people. The journey of a hermit stands in sharp contrast to this. Her life is anchored in one place, the place in which she lives. Her travelling is not through an outer landscape but is an exploration of an inner landscape, that solitary place that lies within us all, known only to us; an inner space that no one else can fully share or claim to understand however close they may be to us. Paradoxically, though the hermit rarely travels away from the place in which she lives, her outer landscape, her surroundings, become intimately connected to her inner journey colouring it in unexpected ways. This place and this hermitage are her home. Alone, in this her anchorhold, a word which is sometimes used instead of hermitage, she is both rooted and tossed about by all the waves and storms that are a part of every life and have their roots within us. The word anchorhold reflects this graphically.

The specific place in which this story unfolds, as I have said, lies at the very end of the Llŷn Peninsula, at the tip of the northern 'arm' of northwest Wales: Wales, a land that is part of the Celtic fringe of western Britain. The early Christian Church that developed along this western seaboard has some unique features that grew out of the culture of the Welsh people and are closely connected with the landscape itself. The Llŷn Peninsula is a remote area of striking natural beauty, a beauty matched only by the formidable storms that can transform the tranquillity of yesterday into an elemental furore. It is an area that has attracted tourists and seekers, and more specifically seekers of solitude and silence, over hundreds of years and continues to do so to the present day. Why? As my life here began to take shape I realized how important my surroundings were to the life that was evolving. Through the relative fierceness of the elements as well as the very sparseness of this rocky headland, I began to find the connections between this place and the choice of desert or rugged places made by many of those seeking solitude, a theme that has run through accounts of the hermit life from its very beginnings. One contemporary author, Belden C. Lane, has written: 'There is an unaccountable solace that fierce landscapes offer to the soul. They heal as well as mirror the brokenness we find within.' Among those who have crossed my path here some have touched this same experience, as it has been mine also.

The hermit lives simply, in solitude and silence, a deliberate choice made in response to an often insistent 'call' from God that she might well rather not have heard. Solitude means a withdrawal from any form of social life or intimate relationships, let alone many interests that bring colour to our lives. It even means an end to undertaking specific work or choice of profession. Some have aspects of such a life forced upon them through circumstances that they could never have envisaged and would certainly not have chosen. Maybe the experience of someone who has deliberately chosen solitude might have something to say to him or her. But why would anyone choose a life like this willingly? What is the point? Is it not an awful waste, at best a harmless eccentricity, at worst a self-centred delusion and a running away from the responsibilities of life? Some might even see it as an indefensible luxury, a living as a parasite on the generosity of others. What possible place can such a life have in our twenty-first-century western culture? Our contemporary society is so fast moving, so filled with noise and an avalanche of stimuli and demands that rain down on us relentlessly, that knowingly or unknowingly they come to rule our lives. If you have ever lost your diary or your computer has 'gone down', you will know who are the tyrants in your life. Key words of our culture are of values that are 'relevant', 'utilitarian', 'immediately accessible', 'immediately comprehensible'. It is a culture where activism is to the fore and there is little time or space for the more reflective longer views on life or for taking stock. Juxtaposed to a culture that has this relentless busyness at its heart, the life of a hermit is certainly counter-cultural and possibly a challenge to some.

Unlike the life of a monk or nun who lives in community under a common rule of life, the lifestyle of a hermit is rather different. The great and tested Rules of orders such as the Benedictines, Dominicans or Franciscans have been found to be fruitfully adaptable for many living 'in the world'. Such Rules can be unpacked for those in almost every walk of life and some find great strength in being associated with a monastery or convent.[2] The spirit of each Rule has a strong ethos of its own, drawing people of different temperaments to find their spiritual home through the specific inspiration of that Rule. The lifestyle of a hermit cannot be delineated in this way though if she is a member of a religious order the ethos of her own life will be coloured by these spiritual roots. For each hermit, prayer and worship, solitude and a large measure of silence are essentials, but other than that each one lives and develops differently. As distractions, conversations with others and a multiplicity of demands in her life begin to fall away she soon comes face to face with herself and the deeper questions intrinsic to our universe. At first the intensity of this encounter could threaten to derail her; humankind cannot experience too much reality and easily retain a

---

2 See Abbot Christopher Jamison, 2006, *Finding Sanctuary: Monastic Steps for Everyday Life*, Weidenfeld & Nicolson. This book follows on from the popular BBC TV series, *The Monastery*.

balanced mind. It was soon realized that for every hermit an experienced guide is essential not only as a touchstone but as someone to whom she is accountable. In solitude we do not have the constant discipline of learning how best to live with our fellow human beings positively and creatively. Without a guide it would be only too easy – as one exasperated guide was overheard to say – for the life of the hermit to become one in which 'she does what she likes, when she likes and how she likes', coming perilously close to unadulterated narcissism.

The very term hermit or solitary implies a reclusiveness, a living apart, a certain hiddenness, a life not to be exposed to the public gaze or written about. Yet it is through the writings of hermits and through the faithful records of those who have visited them, dating as far back as the fourth and fifth centuries when the first Christian hermits began their lives in the Egyptian and Syrian deserts, that we owe much of what we know of their lives and spiritual insights. This lifestyle came to be known as the eremitic or desert tradition. I certainly make no claim to any special insights but over my latter years here, despite the remoteness of my hermitage, people have found me out and asked to come and see me, not out of curiosity but as fellow seekers. It seems that through this place and through encountering someone here who has lived for many years in this place and is also questing, some find their own path in life opening up and simplifying. Being persuaded that something that is helpful to others, in however small a way, was being given, I eventually agreed to requests that I should write.

So this narrative was born. As it develops so it follows an evolving life. Questions, maybe thrown up by the earlier chapters, are left hanging in the air unanswered, but some began to find a resolution as the years passed by and are spoken of again in later chapters. Yet answers are rarely the stuff of a questing life or journey of faith. Rather the way begins to open up and simplify through hints and possibilities that each must unpack for themselves if they are to make them their own. Dogma, doctrines and rules alone are rarely the answer to the enquiring mind though they can form a scaffold and common ground that help to hold us to the path and knit us together one with another. Neither are meditation techniques an answer. They may help us to relax and become silent and still but they are always a means to an end, not an end in themselves.

The flow of the narrative is sometimes interjected by quotations from other writings, especially from poetry. These reflect or mirror what has gone before and encourage a time to pause before reading on, giving rein to the imagination. When Bach first wrote two of his greatest choral works, the *St Matthew* and *St John Passions*, he introduced the chorale into the compositions in a new way. In these works the chorales serve, in part, as interjections in the flow of the Passion narrative. They mirror or reflect the preceding aria, and also draw in the listeners as participants, for the chorales were originally congregational. Similarly the psalm that is said between the lessons of, say, Morning and Evening Prayer in many liturgical traditions, serves something of the same purpose, forming a reflection on the lessons.

So this narrative, as has been said, takes the form of three interweaving stories, three 'journeys': the story of this place and its history, my own personal journey lived out here in this place, and the universal journey in which we all share through our common humanity – the human condition. Jung called this, in part, the 'collective unconscious'. Through our shared humanity other lives, often so different from our own, nevertheless resonate with something in our own experience and speak to us.

In everyone there is a solitary centre and a silent place that longs for attention and space. Many are aware of this. Does a life in which silence is paramount have something to say to them that will resonate in their own lives? They too have rare times of stillness within the cacophony of noise and busyness in which they live. Some may even find that it is possible to programme in such times of silence within the relentless pressures of their lives, not just 'making time' for this but finding that it is an essential for them for a balanced life. Many of us lie awake at night tossing and turning, wishing only that we could get to sleep again. There we lie in relative silence, our restless minds chasing thought after thought or an anxiety to which we can see no answer. If only we could still our minds we might be able to get back to sleep or maybe use the time to pray or think with less anxiety. The hermit too is constantly aware of her ever-busy mind and has herself only gradually found doorways into stillness. Her experience and empathy might be of help to some. There are others who, in these times of grave uncertainty and global and financial crisis, of breakdown in relationships and little sense of community, sometimes even of family, find themselves forced to live alone in unsought simplicity. For these, their changed lifestyle is certainly not what they would have chosen. Faced with loneliness and perplexity, the hermit struggles also, only gradually finding that measure of peace and solitude that is of a different quality from loneliness.

Yet it is not only those who through no choice of their own have been forced to live more simply or alone, or else are more pressured by contemporary living than they would ever choose to be. Many make deliberate choices in their lives that alter their lifestyle. They may have a great concern for peace and for reconciliation on all sorts of levels or choose to live simply in their concern for the planet or for the growing gap between the excessively affluent and the very poor, or by an almost overwhelming sense of disintegration around them. Above all there are many, whatever their beliefs or ideals, who know that change must start with them. Nor are solitude and silence an end in themselves but part of our human condition crying out for attention in order that we may become more rounded people and a greater source for good. Ours is a society so focused on the very real distress of many that ways of helping or of problem-solving have almost overtaken the way that we see life, so that we concentrate more on our woundedness than on the wonder of life in itself, let alone on the real contentment which we surely feel at times.

The solitary life, though it may be a road less travelled, is not to be extolled. All human lives are of equal value in themselves and there is no higher or lower 'call' within a life of faith or between any of our lives. For each of us the journey through life is our call and challenges us within our unique circumstances. Whether we recognize it or not, we all have a spark of the 'divine' within us whatever we may understand by this: a recognition that there is something else within us and beyond us that gives rise to what we call our conscience and undergirds our values. For some this is God. For others it may be humanism or some other philosophical outlook on life. Our lives reflect our response to these values and though we may have little or no freedom to alter our outward circumstances, however appalling these may be, no one and nothing can rob us of that spark of inner freedom.

One

Fork in the Road

Yesterday the wind tore at the rocks, the cliffs, the hedges; today barely a whisper ruffles the grass in the field below me. In the Sound the tide race runs deep sucking at the surface of the water but only small eddies catch at a passing shoal of mackerel. This is a compact landscape and seascape yet with a diversity that only becomes apparent gradually with attention to detail. The immediate impact of sky and sea, headland and Island, and their ever-changing moods, intensity of colour and movement in a landscape relatively uncultivated by human beings stirs something in the depths of mind and spirit starved of wide horizons and the roots of human life hidden in the distant past. Perhaps some idealize this as a rural idyll. Yet we do have our roots in the soil. The natural world reflects back to us something deep within our psyches through its earthiness, through the closeness to the changing seasons, the cycle of new growth, of flowering, of fruit and seed-bearing and the decline into autumn leaf-fall and winter dormancy.

I had travelled quite extensively before coming to settle in this remote part of Wales. My journeys had taken me to places of natural grandeur which dwarf the land that surrounds me now. I remember a summer in Switzerland and the snow peaks of the Alps. One evening we climbed the lower slopes through a night so dark it seemed almost opaque, to reach the first mountain hut above the snowline as the sunrise struck first peak then valley, and was reflected a thousand times by the frozen snow. And on descending we stumbled across the first fragile alpine snowbell, *Soldanella alpina*, under the lip of a glacier, a glacier maybe as old as the ice age.

Another year we were coasting in and out of the fjords of Norway when a wild storm blew up. The narrow strait sent echoes ricocheting from side to side like some dervish dance in elemental sounds. Leaving the sea behind us we travelled through an ever-changing landscape to the tundra of northern Sweden. Here the forests with their heavy horned elk, which we glimpsed only once in the shadows of the forest edge, give way to a desert-like scrub where the cloudberries grow. This was a place of almost perpetual daylight for a few weeks each summer and well-nigh unbroken darkness through the long winters; a place which plays on the human spirit, plunging it from elation to the depths of depression as excess of light gives way to unremitting darkness. Very early memories take me back to a day in spring when, as a young child of three or four, I was walking with my mother through what must have been a beech wood in early spring. Above us stretched a canopy of interlacing boughs with the first tight leaf buds just beginning to break. Quite suddenly we stepped out into an enchanted glade of dappled sunlight and all around our feet lay a carpet of wild cyclamen. The colour of the cyclamen and the young green of the leaves against the silver-grey bark of the trees is as vividly etched on my mind's eye as though it were only yesterday.

This place and landscape, this immediate square mile at the tip of the Llŷn Peninsula, does not have the sense of grandeur of, say, the Alps or fjords of Norway and Sweden. There is something more intimate here, hidden from the immediate gaze of the casual observer. Here there are no high peaks, no deserts stretching as far as the eye can reach, no forests or lakes or rivers fed by glaciers or wild waterfalls, at least no longer now with the Ice Age in the far distant past. Everything here is in miniature except the elemental storms and the sea. The rocky headlands, small springs, pools and streams, even the cliffs are friendly enough for the eye to memorize each ledge and stony outcrop. The Sound is less than 4 km wide and even the wide horizon is broken by the Island: Bardsey. The Island dominates by its sheer presence, drawing the Peninsula to itself. Yet seen from the mainland its natural configuration mirrors the shape of the mainland coastal hills and seems unspectacular. If the sea is calm it appears to break the surface of the water like a huge whale motionless or sleeping. There is a unity and fragility to this place which only gives up its secrets gradually. Remote and exposed to the elements, maybe because of this, many have been drawn to this western seaboard down the centuries, drawn by something almost intangible: a gossamer thin veil separates past, present and future here, time from eternity. There is a sense of timelessness, of the crossing of thresholds.

It was just after Easter in April 1981 that I found myself moving into this small wooden cabin named Tŷ Pren[1] which was to become my home for over 25 years. Overall it measures no more than 5 metres square but large windows on every side give a deceptive sense of space and dispel any feeling of claustrophobia. It was remarkably compact and boasted within that small space two rooms and a galley kitchen. A cold tap in the kitchen and Calor gas for light and heat were the only concessions to the utilities of the twentieth century. Much needed doing to make it habitable before the winter. There were telltale signs of water seeping in through cracked windowpanes and obvious traces that I was to share my living space with more than one whiskered four-footed friend with whom I doubted my capacity for friendship at such close quarters. It had been put up as a holiday hut in about 1940 before planning permission had become obligatory, but had long since been abandoned, I suspect for something more spacious or a modern bungalow.

I had quite literally stumbled on this place tucked into the corner of a field, half hidden on three sides by high banks. The sheep fencing on the fourth side had been trampled down so the small patch of land round the cabin was open to predation and overgrown with brambles and nettles, yet not beyond reclamation. Could I make it into a garden for vegetables and soft fruit? The

---

1 Welsh: *Tŷ* meaning house, *Pren* meaning wood.

cabin itself was a poor little place at first sight, abandoned and no longer treasured for its unique and amazing view. But it could be rescued and its potential as a would-be hermitage was obvious. The situation was arresting. Standing barely 100 metres from the cliffs overlooking the Sound, the cabin faced straight out to Bardsey as though pointing a finger of prayer that gathered up all the lives of those who had lived here down the ages, all who came now, seeking, and all that the future might hold. I felt this immediately I stumbled on it, little knowing what I meant by this sense of focus, of this 'gathering in'. Without doubt the immediate focus was the Island and what it stood for, but within this image lay that of the whole world in microcosm. Intuitively I realized that I had stumbled upon or rather that I had been given the place in which I was to be, though at that stage I could not have articulated what I later found to be this microcosm of the whole created universe. Tumbledown though it was, it could still be rescued and above all it was empty and just waiting for someone in search of solitude, silence and space; waiting for someone to love it back to life. I had always lived in relatively large houses set in good-sized gardens. This cabin was tiny but the setting was immense.

The farmer on whose land it stood was intrigued by my tentative enquiry as to whether I might perhaps rent the place, for he had no use for it and was considering converting it into a palatial pigsty! I was quite open as to why I would like to live in such an unlikely place and this did not seem to faze the farming family at all. I gradually came to understand that the people in this area are very tolerant of the idiosyncratic and of most unconventional lifestyles. Provided we incomers respect and do not disrupt the social and cultural life of this rural part of Welsh-speaking Wales most people are accepted for who they are and made welcome. In all my many years here I have never experienced personally the sometimes uglier side of Welsh/English relations. We are the incomers.

Twenty-four years in the common life of a religious community had been a good preparation for the life which I now hoped to explore. The years in community had been both rich and varied: at times life-giving, at times difficult and perplexing. How could such a life be 'easy' if lived authentically? Our community was what was then termed one which led the 'mixed life', that is to say, we followed a basically monastic pattern of prayer and worship, silence and *lectio divina*,[2] manual work and creative crafts, and times of recreation, the technical term used in the monastic life for times of relaxation in common. But we also worked outside the enclosure of the convent in a variety of fields as the needs of people and the Church arose, and we were asked to respond according to the availability and expertise of the sisters. To begin with I felt as though I was on another planet. Almost every minute of the day was regulated and most gruelling of all was the lack of privacy. We were never alone except when we closed our doors at night so dog-tired that sleep came almost instantly. But I had come to learn to lead a life of prayer and worship and if this was what it took then I would give it my best. This was the 1950s when we were fired by a zeal to change the world and never to allow another war such as that we had just lived through. The monastic life was surely one way through which to build this better world.

After 24 years it was hard to step out, to move to the margins away from the corporate life and the sisters with whom I had shared that life and the people I had come to know well through my pastoral work, to step out into solitude. Yet the sense that this was of God, not just for myself but also as part of the evolving life of the community as a whole, had grown persistently stronger as the years went by. There seemed to be a potential for the solitary life on the margins of the community to add something new within our ethos. For me personally it felt as though it was a development of the central commitment to God which had drawn me, drawn us all, into the religious life in our many different ways. Some words which had been given to us in a talk on prayer and

---

2 *Lectio divina*: reading undertaken slowly and meditatively; taking a sacred text and reading it with the conviction that God was addressing you personally as you read.

spirituality kept recurring to me with an immediacy that would not leave me alone:

> A person who prays, maybe someone committed to the life of a hermit, can learn to live at the point of intersection where the Love of God and the tensions and suffering we inflict on one another meet, and are held to God's transforming Love. (Mother Mary Clare SLG).

God, a life of prayer in response to God's love, people and all creation held in that love, had always been the central thrust of what had drawn me to a life built on faith, but I had never found what I was seeking fully expressed through any particular Christian spiritual tradition or any particular work. All were only partial indicators of the way. This grand view of why I thought I had come into the religious life had soon been tempered by the realization of my own need to be changed, my own sharp corners and unhealed wounds, yet from a very early stage in my life in community prayer in solitude had drawn me though I had little idea of how this might be realized or what it might entail. Now in the late 1970s the possibility of a recognized vocation to an eremitic[3] life had begun to open up once again within the Anglican tradition. These words of Mother Mary Clare's resonated for me with something that I had, as it were, always known but that had lain dormant waiting for a touch paper: '. . . maybe someone living the life of a hermit'. What did this mean? What was 'the life of a hermit'? How could I find out, let alone ever dare to begin? Tentatively I began to put out feelers. As the path grew clearer so we began to explore the possibilities as a community, for any decision of this sort would need to be accepted by the sisters as a whole. Eventually I set out to explore this life with the blessing of my sisters.

It is hazardous to be too much alone. To identify that aloneness as 'the point of intersection where the tensions of our world

---

3 Eremitic: life of a hermit or recluse in the desert tradition.

meet and can be held to God's transforming Love', that felt doubly hazardous, almost presumptuous to even think about it. What did I know of 'God's transforming Love' though I had caught glimpses of it in the lives of others and even fleetingly as a gift in my own life? Taken literally the pitfalls loomed large, the sense of inadequacy more than daunting. Was it all a mirage clothed in spiritual language? Yet the traditions of the eremitic life were long and well grounded in healthy godly common-sense terms. It was a way of life found within the traditions of all the great religious faiths and practised long before its 'rebirth' in the Desert tradition and the beginnings of Christian monasticism of the fourth and fifth centuries in Egypt and Syria. What had others found in this life in their very different eras, cultures and expressions of faith?

In our twentieth/twenty-first-century western world, we no longer live in a society like that of early antiquity when almost all were believers of some sort and lived in a climate where faith in God or gods was almost universal. To be a believing active Christian in our age was in itself becoming more rare. And yet, and yet . . . The thirst for things spiritual was very much in evidence, a thirst for a meaning to life beyond the excessive materialism and need for instant gratification so prevalent in our society at present. Many feel as though they are staring into an abyss. Deep in the human psyche lies the longing for whatever we may mean by 'God' and many harbour a great fear that death might mean 'extinction'. Deeper still lies this search for meaning. For me it seemed that at least in part, the renewal of the eremitic life in recent years was an aspect of this thirst. There was a sense of urgency that in a world that was changing so rapidly and seemingly intent on destroying itself, the times were urgent. The counter-cultural intent of monasticism needed to regain its cutting edge.

So my move into solitude began to take shape. After an initial two years of testing in a less remote place and mitigated solitude I found myself, on this spring day in 1981, in this small wooden cabin on the coastal fringe of Celtic Wales.

A solitary neither
Proves nor disproves God.
What we call narrowness
Perhaps is vocation.[4]

Stepping out to the margins of society is more than just a move away from the environment in which we find ourselves. It is a purposeful stepping out of that framework of everyday life and its complex cultural structures. In this day and age in a crowded island such as the UK it cannot but be a relative move to the margins especially for a woman on her own, but even so for me it was a radical move. I felt neither courageous nor self-confident. For most of my life I had lived on the outskirts of a town with open country on my doorstep, so a rural setting was not new to me. But most of the amenities of life which we now take for granted in the West, such as shops and transport, doctors and hospitals, libraries and a parish church, let alone theatres, concerts and galleries, had always been within easy reach, as were friends and family and people to call on in an emergency. Where I found myself now, out of choice, there were none of these things within easy reach. Moreover I had never before lived on my own for any length of time. Pen Llŷn is not isolated but it is remote, which is just what I was seeking. Life in solitude and the spaciousness it offers is just that: solitary, silent and spacious though not all are drawn to the remoteness that I sought. The nearest farm to the cabin was only a quarter of a mile away, so I was hardly isolated or without a neighbour, yet for me it felt like a radical move to the margins. I had never lived in Wales, did not understand a word of the language let alone have any idea of the deep-rooted culture of this land. Here I was with no given shape to my life nor specific tasks such as is normal for the majority of people. To a quite radical extent it was a dropping out of sight and sound . . . into what?

---

4 Thomas, R. S., 1990, 'Insularities: For a Nun on Her Island', in *New Welsh Review*, III, 1.

Some would say it is a running away, others a running towards.
This is the Way he travelled to flee the world;
This is the Way he travelled to return to the world.
I, too, come and go along this Sacred Path
That bridges life and death
And traverses illusion.[5]

Running away . . . running towards . . . Away from what, towards what or whom? Perhaps I had thought that I knew at least in part, and that sense of purpose, however partial, was sufficient to help me to begin and to cloak some of the fears.

On the face of it a solitary life can seem self-centred in the extreme. Yet I had come with a very definite sense of purpose, which in no way separated me from humanity or the whole of creation and which I sincerely hoped would draw me closer to all in drawing me closer to God; *God's* drawing of me, not anything I could do of myself for God, is both the call and the response. If prayer is valid and humanity and the whole universe are inextricably interconnected, then the eremitic tradition, which is primarily a life of prayer, is as anchored in reality now as it was deemed to be in the fourth and fifth centuries and all down the ages. It has never been possible to justify this life on purely rational grounds and never will be, but it can be seen as one way of life among all the others to which some Christians feel 'called'. So I took this first leap of faith into the silence and spaciousness of solitude, and it was as well that I had next to no idea where this would lead me.

Alarm bells rang in my head not withstanding. 'It is not good for man to be alone' (Gen. 2.18). This felt uncomfortably close to the bone, too much like unadulterated reality. But other voices were more persistent: 'Nothing in all creation is so close to God as stillness' (Meister Eckhart).

---

5 Kownacki, Mary Lou, 2004, *Between Two Souls: Conversations with Ryōkan*, Eerdmans, p. 146. (Ryōkan was a nineteenth-century Zen Buddhist monk.)

Those first months and years involved a radical change of gear from the relatively fast-moving life I had been used to, in which we were required to do at least two or three things at once and at speed. Women are notoriously labelled as multi-tasking which is a mixed if essential blessing for most of us. Now I began to live with the clock banished to a corner of the room almost out of sight and little that I had to do except that which keeps body and soul together and learn to become more open to God in prayer. In our twenty-first century lives that central thrust is almost pushed to the margins. At best we make occasional room for it but rarely is it an integrated essential in life. Now here I was with virtually nothing else 'to do'. There was to be no clock-watching, so that a new rhythm could take shape if it would.

The sequence of day and night, the seasons as they followed one another, the challenge of cold and heat, wet and fine, all these form a natural rhythm in themselves needing no clocks or detailed 'rules of life'. How to live in this open-ended rhythm so that it became in any real sense a 'life of prayer'? What is prayer as distinct from life? A life of faith longs to be open to the Spirit, to be guided and sustained by God, to make real the imprint of the living Christ as the Way and the Truth. The cloth of life is woven of the same essential threads for all of us but the contexts vary enormously and for each one is unique. More often than not there is little we can do to alter the givens of our circumstances, yet our roots and our environment, even our genes, never completely decide our destiny. Solitude offers a unique opportunity, under circumstances of rare freedom of choice in which there are relatively few parameters laid down. Suddenly there was no limit to time just to sit and gaze, to listen, to savour, hoping to begin to see with clearer eyes, to listen where before the cacophony of sounds and voices had deafened and dulled, unrecognized then as the welcome distractions that they must have been at times. Now there was time to smell the air and the earth, to taste the salt on the wind and feel the difference to the touch of grass wet with dew or with recent rain. To let the senses come alive in the richness of textures and colours, where normal circumstances had often deadened their immediate impact or, worse still for some, exploitation by others had deprived them of even these 'natural pleasures'. Yet with this sense of liberation came the inevitable feeling of guilt, knowing that so few had the freedom to live in this way. Guilt also engendered by the voices of centuries of Church teaching on the dangers of the senses and the sensual, let alone of idle hands. How many Victorian parents underlined this unchallenged maxim of life: 'the devil finds work for idle hands'.

Alongside this 'freeing of the senses' there was so much to shed and jettison in order to become more open to the solitude and silence. We cannot empty our minds but we can rid ourselves of at least some of the clutter that fills our lives and heads. Much that was necessary, creative and good under other circumstances could become an encumbrance to me now as I aimed to simplify my life and live in as much solitude as possible. So much of what we value in life comes through interaction with others and solitude precludes this to a large degree. Much that seemed essential needed to be relegated to the rich store of memory but given no present access. Material possessions and finance loom large in contemporary western society – mine would be pared down to a minimum, I hoped. Obviously I did need money for my everyday needs and to pay the small rent for the cabin. The community bursar opened a personal community bank account for me and kept it at a level that we reckoned would cover the essentials of my life, but the hope was that I would gradually find ways of earning my own living that were consistent with the solitude. Banks and the use of money were changing rapidly so I needed to keep abreast with the use of debit cards and security codes, but at this stage I certainly did not need to immerse myself in IT, nor did I even need a phone – there was one at the farm in case of emergencies. Communications both between people and in methods of transport were becoming ever more complex and rapid, but not for me, as I would be walking wherever possible or else relying on the local bus. Life could now be lived at a slower pace without all the rush that dogs so many of us. Clothes should not be a problem either after 24 years in the corporate life of the community. But wearing a nun's habit and veil while also tussling with the gales or wading through the mud was hardly practical and, in any case I did not want to stand out, but hoped to blend in as far as possible. In this I was less successful than I had thought, for imagine my astonishment when the post brought a letter addressed to: 'The Sister who lives in the cabin opposite Bardsey. Pen Llŷn'. But that was all, and yet it found me. I had thought I was pretty well camouflaged in what were mostly well-worn hand-me-downs.

A transistor radio kept me in touch with headline news, but I missed having access to a daily paper – or the crossword! Being without a TV was not a problem. The lack of books and music, however, was more of a challenge. I had always been an avid reader and also able to lose myself in music. Now I began with just one shelf of books, which included a few favourite classics, and that was all until I discovered the mobile library, where there were some good biographies among all the romantic novels and the large section in Welsh. The loss of a real library and music was a severe deprivation. But obviously the greatest change was having no specific work or responsibilities or daily interaction with others. I kept correspondence to a minimum and friends knew that I would not be writing or encouraging letters, and that too was hard. Yet the almost continuous conversations that go on in most of our heads most of the time when our minds are not otherwise engaged proved a more intractable problem, and hinged on learning little by little to live as fully as possible in each present moment, and occupying myself with just one task at a time so as to break the ingrained habit of multi-tasking. These are just a few of the facets of life which now had the potential to be distractions or escape routes from the life I was beginning to explore in simplicity and singleness of purpose.

For anyone who has moved house or even for some who are newly retired or whose children have left the nest there are always practical things to sort out as well as the psychological/emotional adjustments. Freed from the tyranny of the clock, the rhythms of my daily life soon fell into place quite naturally. I got up early around 4 a.m. At that hour it is normally still dark and deeply silent. This period of prayer before breakfast became pivotal. Each day obviously involved all the normal household chores. At first cooking and meals fussed me. I enjoy good food and am mostly at ease with my own company, but cooking just for me and as simply as possible was unattractive. I was reduced, at first, to mapping out a menu for the week to ensure that I ate adequately and stopped getting fussed. What strange things proved to be stumbling blocks! My facilities were basic: a two-ring Calor gas cooker with a grill/oven – which was excellent for baking bread – and a small Calor gas fridge to obviate the necessity for frequent shopping. I usually walked down to the store in Aberdaron for a weekly shop and occasionally took the bus 'into town', Pwllheli, twenty miles away, if I needed to do a bigger shop.

Making a garden out of the corner of the field that surrounded the cabin, often in the teeth of a gale and salt-laden winds, was something quite new to me. I had to learn to grow vegetables and some hardy soft fruit without having any idea what varieties might be suitable for this area. One year, to my delight, I found I was offering hospitality to a wren as he set about building a nest for his wife in one of my giant purple sprouting broccoli plants. Alas she ultimately rejected it for another nest built elsewhere. Apparently the male wren often builds two or three nests before the female decides on one. When not gardening I walked the fields and headlands in the immediate vicinity and spent long periods sitting on rocks overlooking the sea. It was a healthy life in beautiful natural surroundings that fed me richly. As the years passed, so the life evolved, and I became less black and white in my views and gentler, as past and present began to become more integrated.

But this is leaping ahead. For now the immediate questions were how to still the ever busy mind, to allow life to wash body, mind and spirit of even its surface overlay? How to become more aware of some of the masks and defences behind which we hide and to face into the reality they hide? We are so adept at filtering life as it comes towards us, of keeping a controlling brief, of the unconscious veiling of our senses and going down the well-worn paths that defend us against hurt and fear, the paths of self-deception.

> In the desert of the heart
> Let the healing fountain start.
> In the prison of his days
> Teach the free man how to praise.[6]

The exploration of that which lies within is a necessary part of the exploration of that which is beyond. This is not to become enmeshed in introspection but to open a window to attentiveness and greater awareness: *metanoia*,[7] a turning towards what is within. For me, both the change in rhythm and circumstances of my life, and the need to shed so much excess baggage, was a radical switch from an over-busy work-obsessed world to what felt like a life of comparative 'leisure', in which I deliberately eschewed activism and busyness. In early monasticism, leisure or *otium*[8] was not only an essential mark of the life of a monk, it was integral to the life itself. Leisure, *otium*, is how the monastic life was described in the early Middle Ages (a life free from *negotium*, of busyness and business). Few of us would recognize this as a description of contemporary monasticism, and even St Bernard, that great reformer and founder of the Cistercian Order, who had hoped to reduce busyness and business to a minimum in the life of a monk, was soon to amend this adage wryly to that of a *negotissimum otium*, a very busy leisure indeed. If St Bernard was unable to live a life of monastic leisure, what hope was there for me?

---

6 Auden, W. H., 1968, 'In Memory of W. B. Yeats', in *Selected Poems*, Faber and Faber, p. 42.

7 *Metanoia*: Greek word for repentance; change of mind and heart of our whole being.

8 *Otium*: word used for a measured leisure essential to a monastic life of recollection centred on God and prayer.

True *otium* springs from an inner stillness and silence, a stillness of the whole person in no way synonymous with idleness. This is not something I could learn or act out, I could only wait for it expectantly and, perhaps, clear the ground: 'teach the free man how to praise'. If it was stillness that I longed for, a cessation of the thoughts and distractions of my ever-busy mind, what I actually found was a battlefield of conflicts – not some esoteric spiritual warfare but the mundane stuff of my – our – human condition with all its instincts and desires, all its 'passions' as these instincts and desires were called by the desert monks. This is the immediate 'point of intersection' of the meaning of Mother Mary Clare's words. 'The tensions and sufferings that we inflict on one another' have their root in our own personalities as we surely begin to realize from a very early age. The unacknowledged, often unknown and unresolved knots in our hearts mar our longing to be open to God and to his transforming work in us, our relationships with others and our ability to live life to the full. This is the first crossing point: not something 'out there' but starting with that which is 'within', ourselves, the person I really am, not an image of myself as I would like to be or think I am and which I project onto others. Who doesn't have either an inflated opinion of themselves or else such a poor sense of self-worth that the distortion is just as great? Very gradually also, there was the beginning of a blurring of the false dividing line between what we describe as the outer and the inner: that which I see as external to myself and that which lies within. All I could do was to grope for the path, to begin to read the road signs, alert but passive. This was certainly no idle leisure but equally it is also not *negotium*, a busyness or business. It is, for most of us I guess, the ongoing work of a lifetime, this shift or integration of the many aspects of our lives.

The shadow of puritanical teaching continued to loom large and to cast doubt over the legitimacy of openness to this interpretation of 'freedom'. The stonier the path, the greater the effort and difficulties and the shouldering of often self-imposed disciplines, the more meritorious the ensuing virtues: this teaching dies hard. Yet here in solitude the only witness to any misplaced asceticism was my own stern inner mentor from whom it arose. That way lies not freedom or a loosening of the bonds that bind us, but self-induced fantasies of a quasi-ascetic life. It was proving unexpectedly difficult to shed the sense of guilt and of foolhardiness which held me back from beginning to trust at least some of my natural inclinations 'under God' rather than to act against them. I questioned also whether this might not lead to a greater individualism which has so undermined the essential common good of our contemporary culture. Yes, each of us is unique with our own unique gifts and difficulties, but at the same time we are a part of the whole. Our well-being and that of the whole of creation is interwoven and interdependent. Yet all around me lay the natural world that seemed to witness to just that freedom: the face of God in his creation, or rather the many faces of God, for to my limited human mind and spirit, creation seems full of contradictions and dualities that appear irreconcilable. Was this also a facet of 'the point of intersection', these seeming contradictions? Were those words of Mother Mary Clare's beginning to take on a different meaning through the life I was entering on in this place? I thought I had come to explore solitude and silence in response to God. What was being given were both of these in abundance, good measure and running over, but unexpectedly there was a further dimension: this *place*. This place was more than the natural world and its vibrant life, more even than its unknown history and cultural roots, the *place* seemed to reflect my inner journey back at me, making me one with what surrounded me. To journey, to set out on the pilgrimage which is the journey of life 'is always a travelling to where I am' (Archbishop Rowan Williams).

Those first years were above all ones of exploration and discovery and of the beginning of shedding of clutter. Each morning in the very early hours as I drew back the curtains I felt overwhelmed by my surroundings. The Island secured by the sea, the changing colours of sky and land as the sun rose behind the cabin and the light began to creep down the slopes of the headland and the peak of Enlli mountain, until it reached the water's edge when sky, sea and shore seemed to absorb the colours as they merged. It was different every morning. These first impressions have never left me, never grown dim. Was this something of a honeymoon?

At first the nights were informed by the days but very soon those night hours leading into the dawn came to have a special quality.

> The heavens declare the glory of God,
> the vault of heaven proclaims his handiwork.
> No utterance at all, no speech,
> no sound that anyone can hear;
> yet their voice goes out through all the earth,
> and their message to the ends of the world. (Ps. 19.1, 3–4 JB)

> From Dust I rise,
> And out of Nothing now awake,
> These Brighter Regions which salute mine Eys,
> A Gift from GOD I take.
> The Earth, the Seas, the Light, the Day, the Skies,
> The Sun and Stars are mine; if those I prize . . .

> . . .

> A Stranger here
> Strange things doth meet, strange Glories see;
> Strange Treasures lodg'd in this fair World appear,
> Strange all, and New to me.
> But that they mine should be, who nothing was,
> That Strangest is of all, yet brought to pass.[9]

9 Traherne, Thomas, 1966, 'The Salutation', in *Poems, Centuries & Three Thanksgivings*, ed. Anne Ridler, OUP, p. 6.

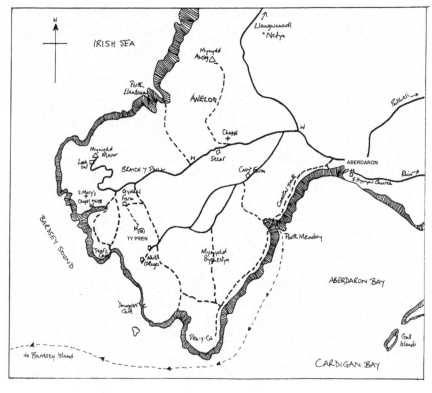

Map 1: Northwest Wales and Uwchmynydd (Tip of the
Llŷn Peninsula)

Two

A Strange Land

When on a train journey I have sometimes found myself passing through places, glimpsed fleetingly but leaving no trace of themselves on my imagination for they are immediately overtaken by another fleeting glimpse which captures my attention and leaves its imprint, colourfully. This place in which I now found myself captured my imagination from the very beginning. Textured and many-coloured, my first impressions began to form and re-form as I started to explore my surroundings, deliberately not ranging far afield, and found a richness which was quite unexpected. I came to know each headland, cliff and field as you would the network of roads in the immediate neighbourhood of your own home town, a broad-brush acquaintance. I found the paths marked on the map and others long overgrown: an old high-banked grassy lane which used to connect the farm a quarter of a mile from the cabin with two cottages half a mile in the opposite direction, which the post-man used daily when letters were rare and delivered on foot. In those days too the cattle from the farm also used this lane morning and evening to drink from the well outside my gate, the same well from which the families at the farm drew water for their own use. The well is still there though largely overgrown, but the water is no longer deemed safe to drink. I discovered the cave on the cliff at Pared Lech Ymenyd below Mynydd Bychestin, which it is said was in regular use by smugglers from Ireland up until the nineteenth century. The strangely uneven ground of the slopes down to the cove below me told of where local enterprise had blasted the rock for the semi-precious stone jasper, found there and on the north coast of the headland at Porth Llanllawen. Below the same slopes there is another cave only accessible at low tide, where I came face to face with a baby seal as surprised to see me as I was to encounter him. He was an oily yellow colour and much whiskered with huge round eyes. I soon discovered how fierce a young seal could be, as he hissed and barked at me in helplessness and fear at his inability to reach the water until high tide would come to his rescue, and his mother would also return after her foraging for food.

On heath land to the south there are the remains of an old settlement of uncertain date, the walls still easily distinguishable standing a few feet proud of the surrounding scrub and the enclosing wall. Walking on to the far point in the same southerly direction – Pen-y-Cil – the view opens up across Aberdaron Bay to Cardigan Bay. On a clear day the full range of the Cambrian mountains stands out, from Snowdonia right down to Strumble Head beyond the Preseli Hills on the southern peninsula of Wales – that southern arm of Pembrokeshire jutting out into the Irish Sea.

Aberdaron lies nestled round the church situated on the seashore itself. The village straggles up the three hills which surround it but it is still easy to visualize the site of the original small cluster of houses round the church in its circular churchyard and to imagine how these were replaced by others long since gone. Circular churchyards were typical in this area from the fourth and fifth centuries indicating the presence of these early settlements. The churchyard would have included all the houses clustered round the church, the surrounding circular wall serving as some protection against marauders or invasion from the sea.

To the west of the cabin, there is evidence of another hut circle possibly dating back to the fifth or sixth centuries and probably connected with St Mary's Chapel whose ruins lie in a flat-bottomed valley between two rocky outcrops with a view straight over to Bardsey. These ruins are the remains of a stone church built on the site of a much earlier wattle and daub chapel. An enclosing wall, strip fields and traces of the foundations of several medieval huts are still visible. It is said that pilgrims setting out on the last and most hazardous leg of their journey to Bardsey prayed first in St Mary's Chapel and then launched their coracles from the cove below by St Mary's Well. The other inlet from which most boats set out was Porth Meudwy –Hermit's Cove– on the more sheltered southern side of the tip of the peninsula. The name itself, Porth Meudwy, is a clue to lives from the distant past in which hermits played a well-documented role. Hermits almost certainly lived on the mainland overlooking the Island (though the evidence for this is inconclusive), and later also on the Island itself where the evidence from later records is more conclusive.

Threads of local history and folklore filtered through to me but I had determined to read little about this place for the first years, hoping that my own solitary encounter with my surroundings would be direct and fresh, uninfluenced to any great extent by too many preconceived ideas. Since the renewed interest in Celtic Christianity there has been a tendency to popularization through a succession of books on 'Celtic spirituality' and modern 'Celtic prayers'. This has led to a somewhat romanticized mystique round the whole idea of the 'Celtic'. There was nothing romantic in what I was meeting in my everyday experience here.

At the top of the headland on Mynydd Mawr stands a small coastguard station and lookout, still manned daily in those early years when I first arrived, before modern technology rendered it redundant. In former years it had helped in the saving of many lives as boats, unprepared for the complex tide race and the rapidly changing moods of the Sound, foundered in these treacherous waters. Even so, in my first years here I witnessed three fatalities through drowning as I sat at my own 'lookout' window. Below the coastguard station are the remains of a World War II gun-fortification round which an uneasy sense of darkness still lingers. Strangely juxtaposed, a precipitous cliff falls vertically to the rocks and sea below, a renowned suicide spot for many years, for it was possible to drive up to the coastguard station and straight over the edge. Now large boulders block off that freefall after four fatalities even in the 25 years that I have lived here.

It took time for my biological clock to adjust to a new rhythm. I began to get up earlier and even hoped to do with less sleep, but have never found I could do that, nor was I able to sustain a broken night. But rising in the very early hours of the morning became pivotal. I had eschewed setting an alarm clock and being woken by its strident ring. For many years in the corporate life of the convent, the chapel bell and its call to worship, prayer and silence had regulated my life. Here this 'regulated life' was a hindrance, as I have said, though the discipline it had taught me stood me in good stead. I soon found myself waking naturally. There was a quality to the solitude of those early hours even when the stillness was swallowed up by the all-invasive roar of the wind, which seemed to engulf my senses. 'Natural' noises are strangely less invasive and jarring than the noise of machines or traffic or even the human voice. Natural noises may drown out silence but not the underlying stillness of the countryside. In those early hours on a dark night, the Island lay silhouetted by the beam of the lighthouse arcing over the sea and Island itself. The actual lighthouse is set on the western arm of the Island and so was hidden from my view but I could see the rhythmic beam of light clearly. Far out over Cardigan Bay, 80 to 100 miles away, the Strumble Head lighthouse winked and, over on the north coast, out of sight beyond the headland, the next light would be signalling off Holyhead on Anglesey. Until I came to live on this rugged coast, the vital importance of our lighthouses had never fully registered, nor the fact that each one signalled to a different time pattern recognizable to all shipping. The scrambling of some of these lighthouse signals was apparently one way in which we had hoped to mislead an invading enemy fleet during World War II. The vastness of the ocean on a night obscured by dense fog or by a storm that whipped up waves to heights and depths that hid all else from view beyond sheer cliffs of water – this was now being enacted all around me.

> There are nights that are so still
> that I can hear the small owl calling
> far off and a fox barking

miles away. It is then that I lie
in the lean hours awake listening
to the swell born somewhere in the Atlantic
rising and falling, rising and falling
wave on wave on the long shore
by the village, that is without light
and companionless. And the thought comes
of that other being who is awake, too,
letting our prayers break on him,
not like this for a few hours,
but for days, years, for eternity.[1]

As I watched and waited, the night hours became central to the rhythm of my life. The quality of those night hours held something that I had not encountered before. Was this something integral to this place? If I had been keeping vigil in some other solitary place would the effect have been the same? In times of retreat while still living at the convent in the corporate life, I had sometimes prayed at night but I had never experienced this quality in the night hours then. Did it have something to do with the fact that I was now alone, in solitude and not just in silence – 'companionless'?

How strange that so many of those early broad-brush observations had to do with human activity, past and present. The beauty of land, sea and sky, birds and creatures, wild flowers and rock pools filled my eyes, ears and spirit. I drank it in whole without attention to detail at this point, but something in my being was taking special note of where humanity had touched this place and left a mark.

My observations of my surroundings had caught me out and had begun to show me levels of attachments, fears and needs in relation to my fellow human beings which it had never been necessary to question before. I had expected that I would reminisce and recall memories, imagining familiar scenes and conversing in my head

---

1 Thomas, R. S., 2001, 'The Other', in *Collected Poems 1945–1990*, Phoenix Press. p. 457.

with people with whom I had lived and shared. I had expected to experience times of acute loneliness, but this was a filling of that vacated place in my life at an unexpected and subtler level. 'It is not good for man to be alone.' Once aware of what was happening I needed to learn to let go of this unconscious seeking for human companionship and day-dreaming, and value the signs left by those from the past as part of the fabric of this place and see what they could teach me. Again I became aware of how this 'fabric' contributed to those night hours leading into dawn: this silence of God's presence. In a town nowadays, it is almost impossible to see the stars clearly even on a cloudless night. Street lighting, traffic, neon signs, all light up the sky so that it is never dark and clear or free from smoke and polluting dust. Here it was densely dark yet with a clarity that revealed the stars and planets and the different patterns they assumed as the earth rotated and the seasons changed. Even indoors Tŷ Pren was totally dark; there was not even the glow of any LED lights which permeate so many of our homes nowadays. I had no mains electricity or even a phone at this stage. All around the world still slept; few creatures, even, frequented the dark, or so I thought in those early days. Men and women had surrendered their domination of their surroundings and slept. The darkness both veiled my eyes and cleared my sight; the stillness alerted me to every sound. It took time for me to feel at home in the clarity of these nights and allow my ever-busy mind to be drawn into a relative emptiness. For passing moments the emptiness seemed inexplicably filled. It was at night that Presence sometimes seemed to cross the natural boundaries of perception.

Yet it was at night also that I sensed a greater awareness of the other side of light, of Lucifer the light-bearer: of light which throws shadows; of death as well as birth, both so often visitants of the early hours; of men not in their beds but committing untold evil or reeling home drunk to create havoc for their families; of homeless people sleeping rough; of those who could not sleep for the fear and suffering in their lives, unloved, despairing, alone. I sensed acutely larger cosmic events which I could not name as I was unaware of the facts surrounding them except through the headlines of the daily news I listened to on the radio. But I was acutely aware of this cosmic impact in prayer. Only gradually was there a partial stilling of these images and the imaginings of my mind, however laudable those imaginations might seem. Increasingly those early hours became more imageless as I forgot myself within the whole world, the world as always present to God. No human being can touch more than an infinitesimal sense of this.

So it was that first summer – at least some of the time. I had barely touched the surface. In some ways I was probably experiencing something of the relief and distancing from pressures that some may feel as they begin on a sabbatical. But for me this was no sabbatical; it was open-ended. Though I was accountable to my spiritual guide and to my community, no time schedule had been mapped out in advance, no deadlines by which 'progress' would be measured, for this was a personal journey and therefore unique to every aspiring hermit.

At this time I was rarely lonely, rarely wrapped up in myself, there was too much to absorb, too great a change of lifestyle to leave much psychic energy for self-absorption, one of the obvious stumbling blocks for anyone much on their own and probably particularly so if that aloneness is unsought and unwelcome.

Increasingly the sense of identification with all humanity and all creation became part of the fabric of my being and with it a growing urgency to enter more fully into this life. Though every hermit life is different, it seems that this sense of awareness, of identification, is one which all experience.

The question as to why so many down the ages appear to have come to *this* place on pilgrimage exercised my mind. Why had they come to this *place* and found here their 'desert hermitage' – 'desert' in the sense of withdrawal to the margins of society? In the early Celtic Church, pilgrimage was not thought of primarily as a journey undertaken as a penance or in order to be rewarded in some way within the context of judgement after death. Often pilgrimage was undertaken towards the end of life, or as a quest in the journey through life, in order to find what was so beautifully termed the pilgrim's 'place of resurrection'. Having arrived, geographically, at their journey's end, they would seek out a holy monk or hermit often living in this place 'made holy' by their lives or the lives of those who had gone before them – the actual lives of these holy men were thought of as having sanctified the place itself. Here, the pilgrim would make a confession of his sins and most probably he would remain in that place until his death. In the legends that surround Bardsey it is said that the pilgrim, having reached the end point of his pilgrimage on arriving at the Island, sought out a holy monk or hermit and was shriven. The rigours of the pilgrimage having cleansed his body, the sacrament of confession having cleansed his soul, he would then climb to the top of Enlli Mountain. Looking over to the mainland on a clear day, he saw the whole of Wales mapped out before him: all his past life encapsulated in the land. Turning then towards the west into the setting sun, he died in peace. This journey towards our 'place of resurrection' was part of the Celtic tradition of which I was becoming a part almost without my realizing it. Yet it is also the ongoing journey of each of us and of the whole universe in which we all have our place. All the potential good, and all the potential evil of which humankind is capable, lies within each of us and our 'place of resurrection' is a way of saying that there comes a time in our lives when we become personally aware of this and our journey under God opens up. For some there is an actual geographical *place* that they can identify with this realization, a place to which they often return for times of renewal or where they may actually come to live. It is here that God's work of transformation is being enacted in each of us individually as part of the transformation of the whole universe. For me, with the increasing sense of solidarity came an increasing sense of the culpability of my own life and the weight of the darkness in the world.

A quiet silent Person may possess
All that is Great or High in Blessedness.
The Inward Work is the Supreme: for all

The other were occasion'd by the Fall.
A man, that seemeth Idle to the view
Of others, may the greatest Business do.
Those Acts which Adam in his Innocence
Performed, carry all the Excellence.
. . . And this at first was mine; These were
My Exercises of the Highest Sphere.
To see, Approve, take Pleasure, and rejoice,
Within, is better than an Empty Voice:
No Melody in Words can Equal that;
The Sweetest Organ, Lute, or Harp, is flat
And Dull, compar'd thereto . . .
O happy Ignorance of other Things,
Which made me present with the King of kings!
. . . The World was more in me, then I in it.
The King of Glory in my Soul did sit.
. . . and Heaven and Earth was there.[2]

My experience of the silence of which Traherne speaks so joyfully was also shot through by the darker side of life both within myself and in the life of all around me. Yet I had never seen, nor could I now see this as a dualistic confrontation of two powers: the 'all-good' and the 'all-evil'. My own increasing awareness of evil in the world and my own culpability was shown me through the light of good and not through focusing on the darkness. The solitude and silence in which I now found myself, and of which Traherne speaks, gently brushed me with the 'Joys of Paradise'. The Desert Fathers describe this increasing awareness of good and evil as a lifelong battle; for me it was being lived out through the down-to-earth everyday nitty-gritty of my life in solitude and silence.

In the tradition of the Desert Fathers the 'cell' was the monk's desert-space where, alone with God, he fought out the battles of the

---

2 Thomas Traherne, 1966, 'Silence', in *Poems, Centuries and Three Thanksgivings*, ed. Anne Ridler, Oxford University Press, p. 26.

{27}

spiritual life, understood in the culture of those early centuries as being the battle with the 'demons', our human 'passions/desires'. Few of the early Desert Fathers saw the passions as anything other than negative, egotistical appetites to be conquered and banished. Isaac the Syrian was one of the few who saw our human condition, including our passions, as God-given at root. His teachings are directed at how they can be cleansed and transformed to become once more the enhancing attributes that they truly are. Perhaps today we feel more at home with the word 'desires' rather than 'passions', a word that has come to have so many overtones.

Remain in your cell and your cell will teach you all. (Abba Moses)

Keep your mind in hell and despair not. (Staretz Silouan)[3]

My 'cell' was certainly situated in a fair place as far as *place* was concerned. Staretz Silouan's words correct any sense of a false idyll or romantic notions that the beauty of natural surroundings might convey to some. 'Keep your mind in hell and despair not.' The words sound exaggerated and almost unhealthily negative to my modern ears, used as I am to psychological 'theories' and a spirituality that lay stress on a positive self-esteem. But his words resonate at a deeper level. They hold the key to recognition of the darker traits of our personalities and how these traits contribute to the darkness of the world as a whole. Once again I was drawn to the point of intersection, the crossing point, where unlove meets the love of God and *can* be transformed. This quotation that had been so key as a catalyst to start me on this solitary exploration began to lose its negative ring and to focus on the positive of 'transformation'.

As I became more at home in my 'cell', so also the constrictions of this life began to bite. There are few distractions here to deflect

---

3 Archimandrite Sofrony, 1958, *The Undistorted Image: Staretz Silouan 1866–1938*, Faith Press, p. 33.

from the singleness of purpose unless I introduce them myself. None of the obvious things that are part of almost everyone's life nowadays in the West: no television (though I do have a radio in order to listen to the daily news and have some idea of what is going on in the world), no shops, little traffic, above all little contact with people. Entering into solitude is a kind of counterpoint to human dissipation, or at least to my own former 'dissipations'. Many interests and gifts, a background and education that had opened my mind and life to the rich diversity of knowledge and cultures, of the arts, music and science, of the faiths of other peoples – so much of this had fed into my life and friendships and work among people as a sister in the corporate life of the community. This is so for all in every walk of life. Now it was necessary to point up the singleness of purpose; to continue to draw on the experiences of life, for that is a strong part of what makes us into the people that we are, but no longer to feed on a rich diet of diversity or to allow myself to fantasize scenes and possibilities other than the given of the present moment. I needed to learn to live in the present, neither in the past nor the unknown future. It was not enough to know with my mind that everything is relatively transient but a matter of living this out through the present. Yet this also is a paradox, as our human attributes of awareness and intuition are based largely on experience and are necessary for our self-preservation.

'Remain in your cell and your cell will teach you all.' To be open to that maxim meant a radical shift of learning-patterns, for all I could do was to learn to become a little more attentive, and how to begin to gather my widely scattered attention into each present moment of time. It was no longer up to me to seek out a way in which to learn new skills nor was I in a position to choose my 'teachers'. The way that lay before me was one of emptying, of shedding, of allowing what each day, each present moment, held and for this to *be* my life, with as little engineering on my part as possible. I could only, to a degree, work on clearing the path. This was certainly not just a passive acceptance but rather an active passivity. Yet it would be foolhardy indeed to attempt this without a sure guide:

someone of wisdom and discernment, skilled in seeing the shape of another's life and the Spirit's workings in that life. Someone who could see 'how the patterns behind the events of today are being *transformed* into the patterns of the events of tomorrow', a saying attributed to St Seraphim of Sarov, a Russian monk and hermit of the nineteenth century. I was enormously fortunate to have such a guide through all the first 10 to 12 years of my life in solitude. It is perhaps not often outside marriage or partnership that we have someone whom we trust to a degree that our often-unrecognized defences come tumbling down. Many of us have several people with whom we discuss different aspects of our lives and that is a gift of friendship in itself, but for a hermit it is essential that she has only *one* spiritual guide to whom she is accountable with as much integrity and honesty as possible.

Having got Tŷ Pren habitable and watertight and made a start on the garden, there were other practical things to work out within the context of being as solitary as possible. What was I going to do about shopping, about going to church, even about collecting my mail and milk, as the postman obviously could not come across two fields to deliver my few letters? These last two practicalities were easy to solve. There was a small outhouse, formerly used as a dairy, at the farm across the fields where the post could be left along with the milk, though even this had its surprises. I opened the door of the dairy one day to be greeted by a very distressed lamb that nearly swept me off my feet in its attempt to escape. It seemed that the postman, having found the lamb wandering motherless along the lane, had caught it and put it in his van and delivered it to the dairy for the farmer to sort out where its mother was from among the fields that bordered the lane.

Shopping was less easy to solve as even then, in my younger days, there was a limit to what I could carry. At first I walked the three miles down to Aberdaron about once a week and bought what I needed. At that early stage I had few vegetables or fruit from my garden. Once a month or so I took the bus about half a mile away which ran from Uwchmynydd into Pwllheli – our nearest small town – for things that I could not get in the village store such as bread flour and cheaper brands of some foods. I baked my own bread as, though I had a very small calor-gas fridge, it was too small to take a loaf of bread and in the summer months bread goes mouldy only too quickly. Gradually I found that this monthly shop was all that was necessary. I smile as I look back on those early days for I used to wear a habit whenever I went out in 'public' and even when at home I wore a headscarf. Some of the externals of conventual life took time to drop away as did much 'religious' language.

Churchgoing was obvious at first as there was only one service: the Eucharist on a Sunday morning. Gradually as I became more and more aware of my solidarity with all of humanity, let alone of all creation, I went to church less frequently and knew that I was one with the local people as I prayed alone. There was also a query in my mind as to whether I should attempt to learn Welsh, as when I did go out among people I realized that nearly all conversation was in Welsh and even every official communiqué was either only in Welsh or bilingual. I am not a natural linguist and Welsh is an extremely difficult language, not only grammatically but even to pronounce, but above all I realized that my inability to converse or understand people helped me to maintain my solitude. So I decided against applying myself to learn the language. I was a stranger in a foreign land. In retrospect I wish I had more Welsh as I would love to be able to read it in the original and have the courtesy to be able to answer people in their own tongue. Obviously over the years I have picked up a little.

Soon darker memories began to surface, memories that had remained so firmly repressed that I was unaware of their existence. At first I found myself remembering with pleasure my early childhood and the years before my fifth birthday. A child's memories are often strongly visual. For me they seemed often to begin at the pool which was a feature of our garden. It was a square stone or concrete pool with a low wall all round it. At each corner there sat a bronze-cast frog of just the right size for a child of five to sit astride its back, warm from the hot sun. These four frogs spat water which filled and circulated in the pool keeping it fresh. But whoever designed the system appeared to have been deficient in the laws of physics, for though the first frog produced a good spout of water whose arc caught the sunlight making wonderful rainbows, the others seemed less able to spout until the fourth produced little more than a dribble. My brother and I spent hours by this pond fishing for the unfortunate goldfish among the water lilies though I have no memory of our ever catching anything.

My memory of the house is less vivid except that it had four floors and a basement. My family occupied two of these and my grandparents – my mother's parents – a self-contained third. The fourth, I seemed to remember, was my mother's bookbinding studio where she did some beautiful tooled-leather work. Each floor was designed for a whole family to live in. It was a light and airy house with extensive gardens, trees and an orchard and every delight for a child to run wild in the summer. Though warm and sunny in the summer the house must have been cold in the winter for I remember there was secondary glazing in all the rooms, the windows separated by white pillow-like cushions presumably to keep out the draughts. I have memories of sitting on the radiator shelves under these windows in the nursery and of the amazing ice crystals on the outer panes. I remember too a large room downstairs which was full of plants: orchids and cacti and other beautiful pot plants with gorgeous scents and colours. I would have been barely tall enough to see them ranged on their tables but this room evokes scents and colours and my mother, whose pride and joy it was. There was a central stone staircase the full height of the house with double doors on each floor giving onto the separate apartments, doors through which I was only allowed to wave to my brother when he went down with diphtheria and then scarlet fever at a time when both these illnesses were seriously life-threatening, so that he had to be barrier nursed by my mother and a nurse, leaving me temporarily motherless.

I am describing our villa on the outskirts of Vienna where we lived for the first five years of my life. My father was a doctor, a consultant physician, my mother artistic and very much the centre of the family and of the circle of artistic friends: painters, writers and musicians who frequented the house. In the 1930s Vienna was still the centre of much of the cultural life of Europe. In many ways it was an idyllic early childhood.

All this ended abruptly in March 1938 with the *Anschluss* and Hitler's annexation of Austria. Those next months seemed to have dropped out of my mind until I came into solitude when the clamps came off, and vivid vignettes of memories surfaced. There was the metallic ring of spurred jackboots on our stone stairs and the subsequent absence of my father from our life. (He was taken into solitary confinement for no named reason, but subsequently released after my mother had obtained the necessary papers for him to leave the country.) I began to remember our move to an apartment with no garden, in the centre of the city, and sitting at the window watching rank upon rank of German soldiers goose-stepping past, swastikas held high and military bands playing tri-umphal marches – so this was why I could never listen to martial music all through the war. I remember too being left in the care of my nursemaid or of the cook for long hours at a time, while my mother was out queuing endlessly for vital papers and passports to enable us to leave for England where my eldest uncle had married and lived since the early 1920s. In September 1938 there was the drive to the airport where my brother and I said goodbye to my mother and a much loved aunt and set out for England on our own. We still have photographs of this leave-taking but not of the sudden emergency when my knickers elastic broke and the tension must have eased. Being by far the youngest passenger on the plane, I was taken into the cockpit and allowed 'to take over the controls'. What strange vignettes are stored in the memory. We were met at Croydon airport by my Irish aunt who spoke practically no Ger-man and by Nanny who spoke none at all, and yet all that stands out in my memory were two enamel bowls in the back of the car in case we were sick and the red, amber and green of the traffic lights flashing past as we drove out of London to Essex to a tiny village out in the country where my uncle and aunt lived.

Then 'normal' memories of things I have always known resumed, but my understanding of those early months in England could only have been that of a young child unable to interpret what had caused this violent uprooting. I was, or seemed to be, a lively, happy child who adapted reasonably well without extremes of distress. Though my new surroundings were so different from anything I had known as home before, yet I remained surrounded by love albeit from people I did not know, who spoke a language I did not at first understand. My brother was less fortunate for at the age of 11 he had much more understanding of what was going on. To compound this he was sent almost immediately as a boarder to prep school so that he could acclimatize more easily and quickly. My father joined us after about nine months and shortly after that my mother also. She had hoped to remain in Vienna long enough to get all our near relatives out of the country into safety. But the political situation escalated too rapidly and she had to go through the horror of leaving, knowing even then that they might not survive. Several of them did not. Once our parents were with us once again it was not long before we moved into our own house in Cambridge shortly before the outbreak of the war in September 1939.

Though I experienced little enough of the horror of what was being perpetrated by the Nazis in Europe, without doubt these early childhood memories of naked evil, and the temporary separation from my parents and all that I knew and trusted, must have played a part in my eventually finding myself drawn to a solitary vocation in response to God's love. And the importance of those words of Mother Mary Clare's, 'to learn to live at the point of intersection where the tensions of this world meet, and can be held to the *transforming* Love of God', held a particularly poignant meaning.

> Never, never again. Pleading remembrance
> Whispers through the gossamer wall:
> *Promise us at least this.* An insisting silence.
> We begin to repair, to overhaul

Soft habits of the psyche, trying to find
Fault lines, trembling earth-shelves,
The will overreaching limits of mind
Grounding worlds in private selves.

Wounds always ajar. In its aftershock
Our earth still trembles and strains.
Tentative moves. Even to probe a rock
Stratum? To map the fault planes?

White noise and quivers. Shifts of geology.
What might be salvaged? Hesitance
Of first mendings. Delicate *perhaps* or *maybe*
Tracing detours of repaired advance.[4]

Having got the cabin decorated and made waterproof, I began to pay attention to creating a garden in the corner of the field in which Tŷ Pren stood. The first bed was dug and planted out with winter brassica seedlings and summer salad seeds and I went happily to bed one night only to be rudely awakened in the early hours. The whole cabin seemed to be shaking, including my bed under me, and a loud rasping noise was coming from a front corner. Leaping up out of bed, I pulled on wellingtons and crept gingerly round the back of Tŷ Pren to be confronted by a very large black and white cow with horns, contentedly rubbing herself against the corner of the cabin. The garden gate lay broken off its hinges and the newly planted vegetable bed trampled and destroyed. Large cows, at that time of night or at any time at that stage of my life here, terrified me, but something had to be done. After a chase twice round the cabin, the terrified animal bolted through the now useless gate giving it a final kick, and disappeared into the night.

4 O'Siadhail, Micheal, 2002, 'Repair', in *The Gossamer Wall: Poems in Witness to the Holocaust*, Bloodaxe Books, p. 121.

That summer was warm and relatively wind free. I began to pray more and more out of doors often just sitting on a rock 'watching and waiting'. The lapping of the sea on the rocks below had a steady rhythm of its own. Sea birds came and went intent on their own business. Occasionally a fishing boat or sail passed through the Sound but none of these held my attention. It was immensely emptying and filling just to be there. For many months I felt guilty just sitting on a rock when the entire world was busily at 'work'. Was I doing anything, just sitting: watching and waiting? Traherne could write from the depths of his experience:

> A man that seemeth Idle to the view
> of others, may the greatest Business do.

But I was not Traherne. I had little faith in my doing any great business. Yet I continued to watch and wait. Watching and waiting for what? I had no answers, only questions, increasing questions with only the assurance to 'Remain in the cell and the cell will teach you all'. I began to sense that I was entering into that long tradition of pilgrim-hermits who had found *this* place of solitude and silence and like me, had sat and watched and waited on God as an integral part of 'all that is'. I had never felt so helpless for neither my mind nor spirit could give me any answers, yet my whole being seemed content to sit and wait.

> Keep your heart clear and transparent
> And you will never be bound.
> A single disturbed thought, though,
> Creates ten thousand distractions,
> Let myriad things captivate you
> And you'll go further and further astray.[5]

---

5 Kownacki, Mary Lou, 2004, *Between Two Souls: Conversations with Ryōkan*, Eerdmans, p. 128.

Three

Wilderness – a Place of Strengthening

Therefore, I will now persuade her,
and bring her into the wilderness,
and speak tenderly to her.
From there I will give her vineyards,
and make the Valley of Trouble a
door of hope.
There she shall respond as in the days
of her youth,
as at the time she came out of
the land of Egypt.
(Hosea 2.14–15)

These words ring as true to anyone on a spiritual journey now as they must have done to the people of Judah and Israel on their spiritual pilgrimage and frequent straying from the ways of Yahweh as they journeyed out of Egypt and bondage towards the Promised Land. They certainly rang true to me as summer began to slip towards autumn and the solitude began to bite.

Those first months and the summer were over, together with the springtime of the beginning of my pilgrimage in this place. I had been let down lightly through an exceptional time of a sense of God's overarching presence and reassurance that 'This is the way: walk in it'. Almost imperceptibly life began to change and I began to enter a wilderness which, though I was prepared in some sense, was of a quality that was new to me. There had been plenty of dry and 'wilderness' times before in my life but no one and no books, however graphically they describe such times, can do so for another. Theoretical or conceptual knowledge in anything in life can only take us so far.

'Wilderness', 'desert' are recurrent themes in the wanderings of the people of Israel; recurrent themes also in Christian writings and spiritual practice all down the ages and across the boundaries of different faiths. The desert experience is as old as the nomadic life, and somewhere in the dim distant past all our roots go back to a nomadic existence. What is it in the wilderness or desert that appears to draw so many and where they find, or rather are given, a sense of God and of the Spirit's transforming of their whole being? Not only do they find this in their own lives, for themselves alone, but they also become more and more conscious of this as part of the transformation of the whole world. Are we speaking of wilderness places that are thought to be particularly charged or sacred? But surely God is totally and equally present to and in the whole world? Yet there *is* something that draws some seekers of God to wilderness/desert *places* that have some peculiar and strange fascination for them.

The desert has a special place in the Christian tradition and in those traditions from which it has sprung. Moses' experience of Yahweh in the Burning Bush overawed him while he was alone and in the desert: 'I must turn aside and look at this great sight, and see why the bush is not burned up' (Ex. 3.3). He *turned aside*, and when God called to him out of the bush, 'Moses hid his face for he was afraid' (Ex. 3.7). In the end, through all the vicissitudes and vacillations of Moses' relationship with God, he was the one who led the people out of Egypt and slavery. But the first 40 years were no entry into a promised land, rather it was a leading not only into the desert but into an inner corporate and personal wilderness through which the Israelites wandered for the next 40 years before they could enter the Promised Land. These were years of testing and failure and gradual strengthening of their resolve and faith.

Elijah too, put to flight by his enemies, by a woman at that, found himself confronted by God on Mt Horeb, the ever present

God from whom he had hoped to escape by running as far away as possible to the extreme limits of the desert, to the holy mountain itself. The outer landscape matched his inner turmoil in a scene so graphic that it never ceases to arrest me. God came to Elijah not in the terrifying shaking of the mountain, not in earthquake, fire or wind, but in a 'still small voice' – the 'sound of sheer silence' (Ex. 19.11–12). John the Baptist, Jesus himself, Paul, all 'were led by the Spirit into the wilderness', the wilderness, the place of wrestling, of testing, of strengthening. What did they mean by 'being led by the Spirit'? How are we to discern this leading and to follow in faith? This is the stuff of every journey of faith, but in solitude where there are so few escape routes or distractions it becomes a very focused question.

After the conversion of the Emperor Constantine in 311, the persecution of Christians stopped and Christianity began to lose its cutting edge. At the same time the Church adopted something of the hierarchical structure of a Roman state. One of the central and life-changing teachings of the Gospels was freedom in the Spirit, the Spirit who was also known as the Advocate. The adoption by the Church of some of the ways of the state led to an added and new set of rules to bind the conscience of the believer. As persecution ceased Christianity was adopted as the state religion and became not only mandatory but also fashionable. It was then that some fled the cities where they felt they could no longer live out the gospel fully, and made the desert their home, first in Egypt and later in the deserts of Syria. Some fled for more mundane reasons, to avoid excessive taxation or conscription into the ever-burgeoning Roman armies. Yet whatever their primary reason for leaving the cities, life in the desert was no sinecure and above all it involved celibacy for those who stayed the course for life. In a society where marriage was the norm and celibacy, even among Christians, still unusual, this was in itself a severe requirement.

Christian monasticism has its roots in the lives of these early seekers in the deserts of Egypt and Syria. It was as if those first hermits and monks sought out an environment that corresponded to the inner longing of their lives. Yet what was this peculiar fascination of the *desert* for these spiritual seekers and does it have any bearing on those who sought out the rugged places of the western and eastern coastal lands and islands of Celtic Britain and Ireland, of Bardsey and Skellig Michael? Here was I on the tip of the Llŷn Peninsula stepping into a tradition seemingly already embedded in these very rocks themselves. Was this some deluded folly or a focused purpose? This is certainly not a terrain that one would normally describe as a desert, but it does hold within itself the challenge of a 'fierce landscape', a wilderness place.

Deserts are desolate inhospitable places. For many miles there is nothing to relieve the eye from the flat expanses of sand shimmering with heat during the day, icily cold at night, bare and inhospitable in the extreme. In the rockier parts arid mountains rise from equally arid plains. Nothing grows except the spiniest of shrubs and cacti and round the far-flung oases a few palm trees. Fierce winds and sandstorms sweep across this wasteland, often drying up what little moisture there is and killing anything green that may have taken a tenuous hold between rocks or in the gullies sculpted by the wind. Few living creatures can survive under these extreme conditions and for humans it poses a challenge demanding extraordinary fortitude and dedication to a singleness of purpose or nomadic way of life. Yet instinctively those first Christian Desert Fathers were drawn to these wild places and were tested and shaped by their very harshness as they followed in the footsteps of those who had trodden this path of pilgrimage before them.

Yet there is also a beauty to the desert. The sand and rocks shine with a spectrum of colours from the deepest reds and ochre to the most transparent shades of yellow and white. In the mountainous parts, deep shadows cast by the relentless sun make for contrasts striking to an eye more accustomed to a gentler light. At the rare times when rain falls, the desert blossoms for the briefest of hours with colours iridescent in the sun. At night the sky is a deep dark dome and the stars seem close enough to touch. The silence and solitude are as vast as the space. Even the soughing roar of the winds only adds to the quality of the silence they cloak. The austerity for those who come to seek God in places such as this is not a self-inflicted punishment but a tool, not an end in itself. It is more difficult to commune with God when body, mind and spirit are satiated beyond their needs. To pray, to become attentive, it is necessary to be alert.

In the desert, living conditions are necessarily simple and spartan. A cave or beehive cell leaves little scope for clutter. The less you have beyond the necessary, the less there is to distract from a singleness of purpose. In the desert, in that pure and clean atmosphere and silence, it is possible perhaps for some to find *themselves*, or more accurately, to plumb the meaning of what it is to be human and who we are, each one of us unique, to find this not only related to our own being but within the context of the whole universe. Unless we begin to know ourselves with greater honesty and truth, how can we relate to God and through him to the entire world? The masks that we wear and the defences we erect all distance us from one another, let alone from God. No life or relationship that is not built on honesty and truth can develop wholesomely. Inevitably it will founder. Yet paradoxically it is the very search for God that opens the way to self-knowledge and the possibility of a growing honesty and truth of our whole being. Landscapes and *place* seem to be integral to this spiritual journey for some as the outer landscape resonates with the inner landscape and they interact to make the journey together. I began to explore what it might mean to journey with, or as part of, *this place*. I needed to allow this to reveal itself gradually, in its own way without my forcing anything or putting boundaries round what I experienced through over-rationalization or conceptualization. A phrase from Annie Dillard's book, *Pilgrim at Tinker Creek*, began to have some meaning for me: 'the world unravelled from reason'.

Some places are spoken of as being liminal, threshold places where boundaries become shadowy or transparent or even crossed. Many have written or spoken of deserts and wildernesses as liminal places; of the sea, mountains and forests as 'liminal'; of wide horizons or lofty, light and upward soaring buildings such as Gothic cathedrals or their minimalist contemporary counterparts. Others speak of caves or small dark spaces where natural light is excluded, reducing sensory perception and the distraction this can involve for some. Liminality, maybe of a place or space, is where a spark may flash across a threshold momentarily, sometimes even persist and ignite to become a flame, a fire. The symbolism of fire and flame is as strong as is that of wilderness. St John of the Cross uses it to great effect. He describes the sequence when a log of wood is put on a fire. First of all it splutters and gives off steam, before gradually becoming blackened and charred, and only then does it at last catch fire and burst into flame. The fire increases in heat, until finally, the log is totally transformed. At Pentecost the gift of the Spirit to the shocked and grieving disciples was 'as tongues of flame' in whatever way we interpret this – an anointing with fire. This passing through fire leads into a new level or quality of life.

Tribal peoples, and the cultures of those whom we disparagingly call 'primitive peoples', have a rich store of stories, songs, dances and initiation rites in which boundaries are crossed. Their oral traditions passed down from generation to generation hold in themselves this sense of life as a continuous journey, life lived on thresholds continually crossed, which lie, as it were, embedded in the land. The land itself is experienced as being inherently a liminal space to which rites of passage are closely linked. This perception is natural, unquestioned and fiercely guarded from prying strangers. There is a living, 'dancing' interplay between the people and their land. This seems to be most marked in cultures with a strong oral tradition such as the Australian Aboriginals in their songlines, the Bushmen of Central Africa, the nomads of South America and many others. Nearer home on the Celtic fringe of Britain, oral traditions to this day remain an integral part of the culture, at least in the more remote rural areas. The Hebridean Islands have their ceilidhs or evenings of storytelling. Here in Wales the Bardic tradition is still vibrantly alive, celebrated now, it is true, in a nineteenth-century form yet retaining something of the sense of the liminal inherent in this land. There are still many eisteddfodau both national and local, especially in the more Welsh-speaking areas of the land such as here on the Llŷn Peninsula. The language not only preserves the tradition but also reworks it from generation to generation allowing it to develop and evolve. Cultures with a predominantly written tradition sometimes seem to have a much-impoverished sense of communion with the land and the earth, the sea and the sky. When used in its starkest and purposefully most unimaginative form as in legal documents, the written word can often portray the world in sharply analytical terms which divides spirit from matter or inner from outer and certainly head from heart. John O'Donohue went as far as to say: 'what is nearest to the heart is often furthest from the word.' Purely factual expression can seem to delineate but may also separate rather than communicate and interpret, depending of course on what one is trying to convey. In cultures with a living oral tradition the words are reinterpreted by each generation and mediate between seeming opposites, building bridges. Yet in all cultures the arts, especially poetry, pass back and forth across boundaries through fantasy and image.

> *Poets* (like *Angels*) where they once appear
> *Hallow* the *place*, and each succeeding year
> Adds *rev'rence* to't, such as at length doth give
> This aged faith, *That there their Genii live.*[1]

The steady spread of urbanization has quite literally obscured the 'song-lines' of the land by building over them and covering them not only with concrete but with a thick layer of pollution: pollution in its widest sense not just of chemicals but of noise, clutter and speed, changes too swift for many to retain their equilibrium and sense of well-being. It is much harder for some to have a sense of the holy in the heart of a city or a town, though for others this

---

1 Vaughan, Henry, 2004, 'To the River Isca', in *Selected Poems*, ed. Anne Cluysenaar, SPCK, p. 27.

ability is enhanced by the very closeness of their fellow human beings often struggling to survive. Does this point to a longing, a nostalgia for an intimacy with the living land and our primeval roots of which we still have a stored imprint in our imaginations and folkmemory as part of our collective unconscious? Have I, and the long line of seekers before me, come to *this* place because we find inherent here both something of the wilderness austerity and a particular sense of the liminal?

As I sit and gaze, watch and wait or walk the headland round about me, I become increasingly conscious that I am beginning to listen to, respond to, the whole of the life of this *place*. I seem to be drawn into a different dimension of perception through the solitary and silent ambience of my life in *this* place. At the same time, I am aware that I am taking a great risk, for this change in perception may threaten what appears to have been a reasonably well-adjusted self, adapted to life in the twentieth century. Or was it? Yet if it crumbles, what will emerge in its place and will my psyche be strong enough to emerge wounded but not felled? This is a place of *encounter* where there are glimpses which illumine the crossing of seemingly impermeable boundaries: spirit from matter; head from heart; myself from the living creatures round me; my humanity from all humanity, and the 'life of all that is' in relation to God; time from eternity. These words from Traherne once again:

The World was more in me than I in it.

. . .

Heaven and Earth was there.

The living world was not just present around me, but through its intimate presence was it becoming a part of me and I of it? Life emerges nowhere more fully or deeply than in the exchange over thresholds crossed. Is not being in love the commonest and most universally known of just this crossing of a threshold, when we lose ourselves in another? And prayer: the gaze of contemplation in which God is always the initiator, is not that also a crossing of a threshold? In both of these we live from within ourselves with that which is 'without' or 'other', separate, yet the boundary becomes permeable. I began to realize that as I allowed my life to flow more freely, neither avoiding the fears that were surfacing nor trying to rationalize nor interpret them too readily, so some of what I experienced as seemingly irreconcilable dualities in life began to lose their hard boundaries of demarcation. My deeply held faith in the idea of the divine as somehow incomprehensibly embracing both good and evil was now giving way to the God who *actually transcends them both and enfolds them in a unity.* The dualities were losing something of their hold and their hard boundaries were softening. This is echoed as I look out now over land and sea. Mist is rolling in. The Island has vanished, the headland is just a shadowy outline and there is no sense of distance or differentiation. Each change of mood of the elements brings with it something of the living world's spoken word. Does this world also in some way apprehend Presence and transformation? Are we both, or rather, is the whole of which all of us are a part, is this charged with exchange and encounter?

The monk or hermit in his life of *otium,* and deliberate eschewing of busyness, a hermit in her life in this exposed yet beautiful place in which there is nowhere to go to escape from that which lays her bare, both have quite deliberately 'chosen' to be there. This drawing apart from the world of *negotium, busyness* and business, opens up the possibility for the spiritual journey to be more attentive to 'this world' of time and space, and even to 'eternity'. Others would call this an openness to earth and heaven, others still, to that which already is and yet is still to come: the eschaton, the eventual end and consummation of the whole universe. Yet to some it will remain a running away. Quite consciously the monk occupies a liminal space: a standing between two 'worlds'. Yet even this has a strongly dualistic ring which is why, for me, that phrase 'the point of intersection/the crossing point', carries so much meaning: encounter – communion – exchange, a bridging place, one undivided world.

Why would anyone in their senses embark on a life which is so full of pitfalls and forgoes so much that is not only pleasurable but good? Yet a path which holds for some the way of faith and hope and love needs to be explored and love is indissolubly *both* joy *and* pain: a bright sadness. This is almost incomprehensible to our finite reasoning minds and our negative fear of pain and its potentially destructive power, but perhaps we can catch a glimpse of what may lie beyond our understanding, a glimpse of a different dimension.

We come from God. When we are conceived we fall, as it were, out of eternity – where there is no 'time' – into time and space and matter. The psalms so often articulate in words the longings of humanity; a longing for something lost yet not for ever; a nostalgia at heart's centre. The language of the psalms does not obfuscate or conceptualize but rather clarifies and enhances the creativity of the imagination.

> You yourself created my inmost parts: you knit me together in my mother's womb . . .
> My frame was not hidden from you: when I was made in secret and woven in the depths of the earth.
> Your eyes beheld my form, as yet unfinished: already in your book were all my members written.
> As day by day they were fashioned: when as yet there was none of them.
>
> (Ps. 139.12, 14–16)

From birth we 'experience' separation. Our whole life is a journey which we travel towards a restoration of that unity in God from which we 'fell' into time and also of that unity with one another and of all creation. Each of us, uniquely, is 'created in God's image', and makes our own journey within the 'journey' of the whole universe, a journey in which we are being both formed and transformed, 'into his likeness: a new creation'. The first chapters of Genesis resonate with images that mirror back to us this sense of life's journey. It is as though the 'Way' is imprinted in our very be-ing waiting to be recognized, discerned and followed through, the beginning of the crossing of the threshold between our longings and their fulfilment.

Henry Vaughan was able to recall something of what he 'knew' as infant innocence:

> Happy those early dayes! When I
> Shin'd in my Angell-infancy.[2]

For me there was little sense of a lost innocence recalled but per-haps there was a whisper of the journey and its End.

'Remain in your cell and your cell will teach you all.'

---

2 Vaughan, 'The Retreate', in *Selected Poems*, p. 71.

Four

Outer Landscape – Inner Landscape

The weeks and months and years began to pass. For those first eight years or so, I saw few people apart from the local folk I came across on my walks or shopping expeditions. Twice a year I went to see my ageing mother who now lived independently in part of my brother's family home. Every few years I spent a few days at the convent and one or other of the sisters came once or twice a year to see me here. This keeps alive a real sense of our mutuality and commitment to one another. This can have a parallel in a parish also where commitment to one another is strong and many single or lonely people may sometimes find the family they lack. The hermit living on the margins of the corporate life hopefully contributes to the whole community by her life of prayer, while the support and care of those living the corporate life help to give the hermit a sense of belonging and the courage to persevere as she explores her solitary path. These visits had an added benefit for me in that the sisters brought up stores which helped me with my shopping, especially of heavy or bulky goods like bread flour and tins. Yet my central sense of belonging became increasingly one of being part of all humanity and the whole of creation, though within this larger context the community of faith, my religious sisters, my family and friends, remained and remain anchorholds of prime importance to me.

Of great importance also was the close contact with the wise and experienced nun who was my spiritual guide and who continued to help to open up the journey for me. It is rare to find someone with whom we can feel so at ease that there are few if any barriers to the degree of honesty and truth we are able to share. I was fortunate to have someone who was all these things for me. Yet my guide did not impose her will or her particular way but left me free to discover my own path. It is not necessary for someone who is in the position of a spiritual guide to a hermit to have actually lived this life, but it is necessary, I believe, that he or she should be living the contemplative life or have had many years of experience of listening to those who are living this life. Everyone has the gift of contemplative *prayer*, but the contemplative *life* is one that is ordered in such a way as to best encourage this prayer through the well-tested means of the monastic traditions down the ages. In the contemplative *life* the life itself is also the work of those living it within the context of *otium*, monastic 'leisure'. It is rare for a contemplative community to take on a specific corporate task or role involving people 'outside' the community other than through hospitality. Sadly, in this present age, *otium* is something hard to maintain in any context.

The place of the spiritual guide for the would-be hermit has always been seen as crucial. There is no one of any self-awareness who does not recognize the fickleness of our hearts and the ease with which we, wittingly or unwittingly, deceive ourselves. In solitude there are not the daily contacts with others who often reflect us back to ourselves, so self-deception is all the easier. The tradition of the spiritual guide for the hermit goes back to the Desert Fathers and has been carried through to the present day. In the early centuries of the desert tradition, those seeking to live as hermits often began their quest in a small group – a lavra – the precursor of what later became a more organized early form of the monastic life. These groups tended to form spontaneously round an abba – a father in God – who would be someone of tested wisdom and holiness. Many of what we have come to know as the *Lives* and *Sayings* of the Desert Fathers are descriptions of the lives and teachings of these 'Wise Old Men' – or very occasionally Desert Mothers, though these were few and far between in an age that was predominantly patriarchal. Their advice is as fresh and incisive now as it was then, and is often couched in a form that seems paradoxical if not anachronistic. There are few actual 'answers'.

Often humorous and always intensely human, they taught through example, through stories, through compassion, drawn from their personal experience of the universal human condition. Many were uneducated and almost certainly were unable to read or write. But some were well educated and had held responsible positions in the towns and cities from which they had come. These were articulate people able to find words and pithy sayings through which to express the life they were living and to teach and help newcomers to find their own path. It is very apparent that they had an intimate knowledge of the Scriptures. There are frequent quotations especially from the prophets and the Gospels, the Pentateuch and some of the writings attributed to St Paul. The recitation of the full Psalter was integral to the rhythm of many of their lives. Great store was set on learning passages of the Scriptures by heart, especially for those who were illiterate. The teachings of these 'Wise Old Men' are full of pithy anecdotes which go to the heart of the temptations, passionate or instinctual desires, self-regard, self-deception and self-justification with which we defend and mask our vulnerable selves and which come between us and a more honest and truthful life without which relationships with our 'neighbour' and with God cannot deepen into true love. A sense of true compunction – the state of one who is pricked to the heart – was central to the transformation of life that they sought but it was always tempered by mercy, God's mercy and the mercy they showed to one another and to themselves. This conjunction of compunction and mercy they called *penthos*, the piercing of the heart often associated with the 'gift of tears': a deep sense of sorrow and wonder at the magnanimity of God.

The figure of the spiritual guide appears consistently in all the major religions of the world: Buddhism, Hinduism, Sufism and, of course, in the Hasidic tradition of Judaism. Within Christianity, in the Russian Orthodox Church the staretz is comparable to the abba of the desert in that once again he or she is recognized by an intrinsic wisdom and holiness acquired after many years within the monastic life, often as a hermit. As in the desert, the disciple is schooled to live a truly ascetic life as a means to an end, not an end in itself. Going to extremes was discouraged and viewed with suspicion; the emphasis was rather to learn to laugh at oneself and certainly not to take oneself too seriously, and to follow the ways of gentleness and compassion through which love can shine. The staretz, having gone through the 'same' school of fire and water, may be given an insight into the life and essential being of the disciple. This can open up the next step of the journey in such a way that the disciple discovers this for himself. There is a reported conversation of St Seraphim of Sarov that goes to the heart of the role of the staretz. (Seraphim, a Russian Orthodox monk and hermit of the nineteenth century, lived deep in the forest of the Russian interior. These forests were the Russian equivalent of a fierce landscape – a desert place.)

> The visible pattern of every single life is of God's choosing. We only have to become conscious of it, follow it courageously, and see that we don't distort God's intention. No two leaves on a tree are perfectly alike. Neither are any two lives. Everyone must strive to fill this unique life of his own with a love of God so constant and so great that it flares up into a luminous love of man. Listen, my joy, we . . . must learn to feel, discern and understand. This only comes through years of reflecting on good and evil. Then we see things good and bad, in the light of God's wisdom: and then we develop the gift of true discrimination without which no one dare guide others . . . *Try to see how the pattern behind the events of today is transformed into the pattern behind the events of tomorrow.*[1] (italics mine)

The parallels in a poem by the eighteenth-century Zen Buddhist wandering monk Ryōkan struck me forcibly:

---

1 Beausobre, Julia de, 1945, *Flame in the Snow*, Constable, p. 118.

Cling to the truth and it becomes falsehood;
Understand falsehood and it becomes truth.
Neither accept nor reject either one.[2]

How did these patterns of life lived so long ago and in such different cultures fit with the early Christian seekers of solitude in these
Celtic parts and filter down through the centuries to the present
time? I was still not ready to read and augment my own small experience with that of those others of whose presence I was becoming ever more deeply aware, but whose personal lives I had not yet
explored. First I needed to get to know more intimately the earth
and sea and sky which were the texture of this place, and above all
I needed to find out a little more of what I meant by 'space', the
third of the three aspects, solitude, silence and space, that I had
thought I had come to find.

Very gradually I became familiar with my environs in greater
detail. The broad-brush acquaintance was being filled in with a
spectrum of colours and detail largely hidden from an inattentive
eye. I discovered the sheltered banks where the first celandine of
the spring shone, golden petals catching the light through the dead
bracken of the winter. The first primroses grew along the damp
edges of the pools in the less well-drained fields where they were
sheltered from the prevailing winds. Bumblebees emerged from
tiny holes in the banks. On another bank even smaller holes housed
clusters of a small bee like a honeybee in miniature. The sheets of
bluebells that pushed their way through the brown carpets of dead
bracken caught the light and turned an intense purple against this
unusual background. In the late summer, meadows that had es-
caped the plough and fertilizers sprouted field mushrooms glistening with dew in the early sunshine at dawn. In the winter the ex-
otic looking blewit mushroom augmented my diet. I gather that a
few people are allergic to blewits, so cook them well and approach

2 Kownaci, M. L., 2004, *Between Two Souls: Conversations with Ryōkan*,
Eerdmans, p. 148.

them with care. Had I not come across this mushroom before, I would certainly never have risked eating it. If colour is anything to go by the blewit surely warns of danger with its violet-blue cap and gills and handsomely striped stalk; perhaps the warning is aimed at other creatures rather than us.

I discovered a badger sett on the very edge of the cliffs overlooking Cardigan Bay. In the spring the badgers appeared to have a great spring clean and all the winter bedding was thrown over the cliff, presumably to be renewed before the birth of the new generation of cubs. A cliff edge seemed the strangest place to find a badger sett. It was as though we had hunted and persecuted these handsome creatures so relentlessly that they had moved to the very brink of the land. I became used to the eerie cry of vixens at night but was unprepared for the unearthly yowls and screams that woke me from a deep sleep once. It seemed as though two creatures, whose sounds were totally unfamiliar to me, were fighting it out to the finish just over the bank behind Tŷ Pren. True, I had noticed some exceedingly evil-smelling excrement in the garden the day before, which had also mystified me. Next morning on my way to collect my milk from the farm outhouse, I nearly stumbled over the most beautiful if fierce looking skunk-like creature lying dead across the path. A polecat, something I had never seen before.

Even less pleasant to me were the adders that lived in the south-facing banks of the garden and made their presence known curled up in the sun or gliding noiselessly about their business. It took me a long time to come to terms with these close neighbours, so much so that I got in touch with the Pest Control department of the County Council in the hope that they could advise. There was a long pause on the phone after I had spilled out my tale of woe before the man on the other end of the line said: 'What was it that you said you had in your garden, madam?' And then came some reassuring advice: that snakes hate the feel of slug pellets on their skins and that though it would do them no harm it would send them off. As the years have gone by it looks as though these silent, sinuous neighbours prefer a habitat further from daily human contact so let us hope both they and I are now content. That summer I got through an unusual quantity of slug pellets, so deeply rooted was my instinctive fear of snakes. The shop in Pwllheli must have marvelled at the number of slugs in my garden. Adders are actually beautiful creatures with their zigzag markings the length of their backs. Gradually I came to welcome them but not if they came too near to my door or when they slid under the cabin. They are actually never very large, so from that point of view they are less startling than the bright green grass snakes that frequented the compost heap. But I was already familiar with grass snakes and knew they were harmless and excellent to have in a garden with their enjoyment of a good meal of slugs. So also were the toads that thrived and bred in the damp patch of land that bordered the well outside my gate. There were slowworms too, some a bright gold that shone in the sunshine, and their near relatives, the lizards, with their red underbellies. When digging in the winter I found them hidden under the surface of the soil where they 'played dead'. On the headland of Mynydd Mawr there was a pool where newts spawned and bred each spring, leaving the water when they reached maturity.

I also began to be able to read some of the signs of my environs: those that indicated a probable change in the weather or foreshadowed the change of the seasons. How the phases of the moon affected not only the tides but also the time for planting seeds, depending on whether they were root crops or grown for their leaves or flowers. This sort of knowledge had not figured in the Natural Sciences I had read at Cambridge. Many would say they were old wives' tales, yet the farmers who worked with the seasons and the land, as they had understood it for generations, wove this knowledge into that of modern twenty-first-century farming methods. Certainly this mixture of ancient farming lore and new technology seemed to bring results.

Yet these were not the only things I learnt as I walked the cliffs and sat on a rock, gradually becoming more aware, more attentive, instead of living with the greater part of my attention absorbed by the myriad thoughts that crowd our heads habitually. Every square inch of ground was alive with creatures and plants, some so tiny that I would never have noticed them before. Yet even their lives were not entirely independent of human interference, since they either thrived or foundered according to whether our husbandry or neglect of the land touched on the viability of their habitats. Each was unique; each had its own life cycle, some very selective and only able to thrive where the soil was rich or the soil was poor, sandy or heavy with clay. Some were ubiquitous, others rare, all of which I had always known, of course, and was part of my enjoyment of the abundant diversity of the flora and fauna of the earth. But now that I was becoming less distracted by the kaleidoscope of images that so richly fills our minds every waking moment of our lives, there was space to sit and gaze and wonder in a less scattered way. This area is designated as one of special scientific interest and there are species that are carefully guarded against the ever present threat of extinction, but for me my natural surroundings were integral to the whole of my life and not primarily focused on the rarity of some of the plants or creatures.

Yet I felt uneasy. Was this sort of attentive awareness not just another way of filling my mind with new distractions from the single-pointed life of solitude? Intuitively I knew that this was not so, but rather that it was part of both the solitude and the silence and enriched these. I was not tempted to explore the minutiae of the wildlife around me but marvelled at its amazing diversity. All this was part of the living world at the heart of which was the living Spirit *in this place*, forming and transforming life shot through with the life of God. In another place and a different context and life, single-pointedness would have another texture. For me as I became accustomed to my surroundings this was not a world dominated by 'things' that assert themselves and demand our attention but rather this place was just itself, demanding nothing *from* me. Laying it out in this way, I knew that it was not another yet more subtle distraction though it had that potential, but rather that it was an integral part of this place and this space in which I was to discover whatever lay in store for me.

To learn to love is also to learn to respect and to value. In an overly busy fast-moving life, how much had I missed of the world around me? How much had I filtered out unconsciously or of necessity in order to live at the pace and with the concentration on the limited sector of life that had been required of me? In part this may be our own deliberate choice but, more often than not, do we give it any thought, are we aware that however limited the choices seem to be, no one and no situation can completely take over our lives? By coming here I had made a deliberate choice that gave the opportunity to live as fully as possible within this given *place*, this given *space*. In my ignorance I had not begun to realize where these two aspects, *place* and *space*, overlapped and interacted with my own inner being, or what I meant by space as opposed to place.

Place: its three-dimensional linear demarcation and its geographical and physical location are but the surface of its richness. But *space*: was this synonymous with my understanding of *place* or at least a particular aspect of it? The wide horizon, the open sea, the untenanted fields and headland and always the potent presence of the Holy Island which is Bardsey, was in part the *space*, which gave to my whole being the freedom to expand and breathe and allow so much detritus to fall away. This was a gift beyond all my expectations. This was the given space in which I now lived and breathed and found my being. The two, place and space, overlapped but I soon began to recognize that the space was limited by the extent and flexibility of my imagination, my memories and previous experience of life and my 'flow of consciousness'. All these permeate our perception without our realizing. But this life and this *place* were changing and reshaping my imagination and therefore my responses and the integrity with which I was learning to live – at least I hoped this was so. This place was beginning to change and reinterpret my understanding of my inner space. The inner landscape or space and the outer landscape interplay, and the extent to which they give up their 'secrets' is largely dependent on the overcoming of our fears, which guard the thresholds of both our 'outer' and our 'inner' lives: our survival instinct.

The Desert Fathers were acutely aware of fear as the basic instinct (they would have named it a demon or passion) that holds us back from living more fully, from loving and from holiness. So as I sat on a rock and watched and waited, longing to begin to touch the fringes of what it might mean: 'to pray without ceasing', what it might mean to really begin to love, as I began to treasure those hours of the night before dawn when the darkness wrapped round the cabin and transformed it into something akin to a cave, so little by little the bonds of fear – not acknowledged or even known – began to loosen their grip slightly. This was no linear journey up the 'spiritual mountain' but just the stuff of ordinary everyday life with all the setbacks and frustrations that is life. Life has a spiral pattern and the way is as often down as up, snakes and ladders.

I began to hit times of acute loneliness; long periods of doubt of the authenticity, let alone the value, of the hermit life. Frequently the grass beckoned greener over the bank and it seemed to me that perhaps I had 'fulfilled', or rather that God had accomplished in me, that which he had wanted to teach me in solitude in order to prepare me for the next task. Each possibility seemed more plausible than the last and in a very real sense good in itself. Each built on my life-long interests and concerns, such as medicine and the poor and underprivileged. HIV/AIDS was much in my mind. Perhaps these first years in solitude were all a preparation for work in this field. What a laudable idea! That particular one lasted for some weeks before I recognized it as yet another temptation, another avenue of escape from the nitty-gritty of learning to put one foot in front of the other through the lifelong journey of integration, transparency and transformation which for me, it would seem, was to be in solitude.

If a trial comes upon you in the place where you live, do not leave that place when the trial comes. Wherever you go you will find that from which you are running is there ahead of you. (Anonymous Desert Father)

Remain in your cell, and your cell will teach you all.

But as always, the teaching was compassionate and tempered with mercy:

> A brother asked one of the Old Men: 'What shall I do? This nagging thought obsesses me: – "You cannot fast and you cannot work, so at least go and visit the sick, because that at least is a loving thing to do".' The Old Man, recognising that the devil had been sowing his seeds, said to the Brother, 'Go. Eat, drink, sleep, *just do not leave your cell*.' (italics mine) (Anonymous Desert Father)

There are few 'happenings' here round this small cabin apart from those in the 'natural' world. During one particular summer I could well have done with less even of these. It was still early in the year and the weather swung between a more settled summer pattern and the unpredictability of April and the storms that could blow up with little if any notice. All was quiet as I went to bed and the sky was clear and heavy with stars; there seemed hardly a space between them. I lingered at the window, watching the Island as it gradually soaked up the gathering darkness and became a silhouette against the sky.

Early to bed, I fell asleep instantly only to be woken by an enormous crashing explosion and light filling the room. Crash followed crash as I leapt out of bed feeling less than courageous. Thunderstorms had been my nadir from a child. Here there was nowhere to hide away and no one with whom to feel safer. Sleep was out of the question as crash followed crash. Switching on the light (by this time I had a small windmill which powered a battery sufficient for electric light) would have been unwise as electricity and lightning are an explosive mix and I did not know the vagaries of power generated by a battery. I drew back the curtains. The scene that greeted my eyes both terrified me and held me spellbound. The Island now was silhouetted by flash after flash of light, not white but green and blue and pink by turn, filling the sky with colour. Intensely white forked lightning dropped from sky to Sound, first here then there then from every corner of the sky. As I watched I was enthralled now rather than afraid, for this was a show of elemental strength beyond anything I had ever seen even in the Alps. In the face of this 'power', human strength was dwarfed to insignificance. As I watched, sheets of lightning swept up the field from the cliff top, until hitting the sheep wire fence it ran sparking along the barbed wire and died. Never before had I been thankful for barbed wire. The storm must have lasted for half an hour at least. Very gradually, the thunder rolled away, rumbling in the distance now almost grumbling that its game of pyrotechnics was at an end. Then the rain came lashing against the window and all looked like only Wales can look when the rain is driven horizontally and dawn is barely distinguishable over land and sea and leaden sky.

Some days later it was so beautiful and warm I set out to a favourite haunt early in the morning before the world had stirred. As I sauntered down the lane past the cottage with the small neat garden and curtained windows, a snapping growling fiend with yellow mane and gigantic paws flew off the wall where he had been lying as was his wont, and went for me from behind. I felt teeth sink into my leg and then heard someone shouting. Too dazed at first to respond, I saw the owner of the 'fiend' catch hold of it and give it a good hiding – alas – and then come towards me full of apologies and solicitude for my welfare and bleeding leg. We had already made friends many weeks previously as I often passed that way and had admired the neat little garden and the handsome lion-like sheep dog, but then it had always been safely chained and only registered its disapproval of me by growling and barking as all good guard dogs should. No great damage had been done to my leg and I made my peace with the poor harassed owner over a strong cup of tea. But it was a long time before I braved that lane again in the early hours before the world awoke. I also thought a booster anti-tetanus injection might be wise.

Yet even this misadventure did not see an end to the vicissitudes of that particular summer. I was having breakfast early one morning, when all of a sudden the whole cabin began to shake, books fell off the shelf and the table began to tilt throwing much of my breakfast onto the floor. It lasted for barely a minute if that, and everything returned to normal. My first thought was of an explosion, but I had experienced the aftershock of an explosion during the bombing raids of the war. This felt strangely different. Better out in the open, I thought, than enclosed by walls that were far from solid. No sooner was I out in the garden than I felt the ground move under my bare feet and the same shaking of all things normally solid and immovable. It was a beautiful morning; only the lowing of the cattle and the obvious terror of the sheep on the headland seemed out of place. The sheep ran aimlessly down the slope and halted, crowded against the fence at the bottom. The cattle shifted uneasily, silent now. Instinctively I thought: is this an earthquake? In rural Wales? I had never before experienced even an earth tremor. Minutes later there was another movement of the ground under my feet, less violent this time, and then another and another; then all seemed calm and peaceful, just another early summer's morning. Had it not been for the books on the floor and the remains of my breakfast under the table I would have begun to doubt my sanity. Not long after Wil[3] from the farm came by and asked if I realized that there had been an earthquake. Apparently it was flashed onto the local news within minutes. Later we learned that it had had its epicentre just down the coast from here and that it had measured 5.4 on the Richter scale, quite a sizeable tremor for this part of the globe. It appears that we live on a fault line but that nothing even approaching that magnitude had been known to occur since records were first kept. Quite a number of buildings were damaged and ominous cracks appeared in walls and chimneys. Yet Tŷ Pren, though only a small wooden cabin raised above ground-level by breeze blocks, was quite unharmed.

Snakes, then dogs like lions, and now an earthquake. I laughed to myself, as this was surely the stuff of medieval hagiography blown up as being the temptations of the devil and the many trials

---

3 Wil: Welsh spelling for the English name 'Will'.

sent to dislodge the hermit and divert him from his resolve. Each event had certainly threatened my less than courageous self, but it was all part of the ongoing life of this area at the end of the twentieth century and not in any sense attributable to the devil or evil. They were to me a coincidence of natural phenomena that certainly shook my fragile confidence but did not tempt me to fancies of sanctity. Events are not metaphors but are themselves. What they may teach us is dependent on our interpretation of what has occurred. The lion-maned dog was only fulfilling his instinctive nature and the trust that was vested in him to guard the house. The electric storm communicated so much of beauty and of the hidden power of the elements, as did the earthquake, so that my imagination and my sense of humanity's impotence in the face of forces quite beyond our control were enhanced. And yet these 'natural' events did so much more than that. They were encounters which crossed thresholds. I experienced a deep sense of communion with this place and this space in which I live. This space, this life and this *place* interplay, and had begun their work in me.

> Some ask the world
>   and are diminished
> in the receiving
>   of it. You gave me
>
> only this small pool
>   that the more I drink
> from, the more overflows
>   me with sourceless light. [4]

---

4 Thomas, R. S., 2001, 'Gift', *Collected Poems: 1945–1990*, Phoenix Press, p. 486.

Five

A Rich Inheritance

It was 11 August 1999, the morning of the total eclipse of the sun. A total eclipse occurs but rarely and I could only dimly imagine how it would be in a place like this with its wide horizons, sea, Island and rocky headland. The highest points with the most extensive outlook were Mynydd Mawr where the old coastguard station stands, or else Mynydd Anelog. But both these vantage points would attract many others from the district. Not only would the local people congregate there but also many tourists and holidaymakers. So I made my way to Mynydd Gwyddel, the headland just below the cabin where I had a favourite 'prayer-rock'. Here there is a slight dip in the ground and the close-cropped grass of the headland surrounds the rocks. Gorse and heather grow in profusion and there is an abundance of flowers and wildlife, insects and birds, for few people disturb this little-known spot away from the coastal path. Here I had an uninterrupted view over sea, sky and Island, and out towards the southwestern horizon from where the shadow cast by the eclipse would be making its approach.

It was a beautiful day, almost cloudless. Cattle were grazing contentedly in the field as I made my way up the grassy slope of the headland to my prayer rock. Sheep were out on the mountain for the summer and were cropping busily below me. The gorse was humming with bees and insects, the golden mass of flowers heavy with the scent of coconut. On the far side of my rock the heather competed for space and was covered with myriad butterflies, mostly tortoiseshells and those tiny blues of the exquisite colour of harebells. There were countless other winged creatures I couldn't identify, and the earth too was a bed of creeping, crawling, scurrying life: centipedes, ants, beetles and woodlice. Wild flowers carpeted the closely cropped turf. Everything here was in miniature as the soil is so shallow. The blue of scabious and creeping forget-me-nots, white and purple clover, tiny ox-eye daisies and pink sea-centaury grew among the bright yellow tormentil. Every season has its predominant colours richly matched by that season's nectar-seeking insects – or is it the other way about? But this was high summer when there is a riot of colours even on this spare headland if you know where to look. High above me a buzzard circled momentarily free of the crows that mercilessly mob these beautiful soaring birds. A raven croaked hoarsely spiralling down over the cliff, while choughs flashed their red bills and legs as they rootled among the heather. High over the Sound a group of gannets quartered the water far below looking for fish. The gulls seemed less organized, flying here and there with no particular pattern to their flight, or so it seemed to me. Maybe their strategy in search for food is more opportunistic, leaving it to the gannets and cormorants to show them the whereabouts of any unsuspecting shoal of fish. The air was so still every sound carried, from the buzz of a bee to the bark of a fox brazenly sunning itself on the hillside in broad daylight.

Very gradually there was a whisper of a change in the air, a premonition of something unknown, unusual, and I became conscious of a tingling shiver up and down my spine. Out to the southwest a dark shadow seemed to be threatening the distant horizon and almost by stealth the temperature seemed to drop and there was a sense of unease, first among the cropping sheep and then among the cattle grazing below me. Within moments the hum of the bees faded away and the gorse and heather stood abandoned by all the busy insect life of barely a few minutes ago. The birds fell silent and disappeared. The sheep, puzzled now by something strange and unknown, sought out the shelter of the rocks and settled down uneasily as if for the night. Even the flowers closed their petals.

The stillness deepened as the dark shadow grew larger and crept closer. The temperature began to drop rapidly now, so that I found myself shivering. Like a shroud, this wall of darkness spread over the Island, Sound and headland until it reached my rock. Without being aware of it I found myself crouching, unconsciously poised for flight. There was a deep brooding silence over all the earth; no living thing stirred. Was this night or was it day? It seemed as though time itself had become disjointed and even distances became deceptive. Then as silently as it had come, the darkness passed over and withdrew towards the northeast. Once again the air took up the warmth of a cloudless August day and all around me stirred back into life as though released from a momentary enchantment.

The Venerable Bede (673–735), in his *Ecclesiastical History of the English People*, describes several eclipses of the sun, for eclipses were rare and noteworthy. At the time when Bede lived they were regarded as terrifying phenomena and in some sense manifestations of the devil or of punishments sent by God, even as heralds of prophesies. Bede linked the eclipses he described with subsequent plagues and pestilences that he saw as following in their wake. He recounts that, 'in the year 538, an eclipse of the sun occurred on the sixteenth of February, lasting from Prime until Terce.[1] . . . In the year 540, an eclipse of the sun occurred on the twentieth of June, and the stars appeared for nearly half an hour after the hour of Terce.' Bede wrote as a man of education. His *Ecclesiastical History* was the first account of Anglo-Saxon England ever written so that he is sometimes regarded as the Father of English history. However, his writings are not quite what we would understand by 'objective' historical writing, as he saw the events that he recorded as an interpretation of God's purposes for the universe. Though he may not have understood quite what an eclipse of the sun involved, yet he was sufficiently versed in stories from the past to know that it was a passing phenomenon. But for the majority of

---

1 Prime and Terce: two monastic offices of the morning.

people, illiterate and unfamiliar with anything beyond their immediate neighbourhood, this darkening of the heavens at the height
of noon, the 'falling' of the stars and the accompanying cold, must
have been terrifying and most certainly a portent of religious enor-
mity, possibly the end of the world. What would have been the
reaction of those early pilgrims in these parts where I now lived,
seeking God in a life of solitude and silence? Or am I assuming that
that was why they were here, that that was what they were seeking?
Who were they? What brought them here, to this headland and
peninsula, to this Island so long known as a 'Holy Island'?

I now felt ready to read and to explore the past and to try and
see how, as an essential part of the present, it is as it were embedded in the very rocks and soil of this place. It is only the things of
timeless value that are passed from age to age and these, though
dependent in expression on the age in which they are experienced
and recorded, are not limited to that age. The things that were in a
sense more ephemeral, that were part of a particular historical time
or culture or society, these we can only interpret falteringly through
the lens of our own age, however much we may think we can enter
into another age and culture. So I became more discriminating but
also more confident that it is possible to glean quite a lot from records of a past age and culture very different from our own.

At the entrance to King's College chapel in Cambridge there is a
permanent display that introduces the visitor to the chapel, to this
amazing place and space. The opening sentence reads: 'We exist
not only in the world but in an image or picture of the world', that
is to say, we see our world in any given age through the signs and
symbols through which we identify ourselves.[2] With this thought
very much at the back of my mind I began to explore and read
about those who had sought out this place down the ages and to
try and discern the thread which links them to us now, in particular to my own solitary life and that of other seekers.

---

2 See Sheldrake, Philip, 1998, *Spirituality and Theology*, Darton, Longman
and Todd, p. 165 for the source of this idea.

Oral and then written records tell us that there were monastic settlements here on Pen Llŷn most probably as early as the fifth century. Aberdaron became a monastic 'centre' from these early medieval times. Here on the Welsh fringe of the Irish Sea and St George's Channel, Celtic monasticism found fertile soil in which to take root and flourish. It is still unclear whether the first monks came singly as early missionaries from either the south of Wales or from across the sea from Ireland, or whether they came in small groups to begin new missionary foundations. Whatever the initial origin of the group that settled in Aberdaron, scholarly opinion now veers more and more towards their missionary impetus. There were no traces of Christian infiltration or settlements in Pen Llŷn before this time, so it seems unlikely that any monk on his own would have known of this area unless he had been shipwrecked off this coast. Whatever its initial provenance the monastic settlement at Aberdaron appeared to flourish.

Celtic monasticism differed somewhat from the nascent western monasticism of continental inland Europe. A typical Celtic monastic settlement, or Clas as it was called in Wales, would normally have a small number of monks who lived under vows and according to certain rules, who formed the core community. The rhythm of their day and night would be punctuated by the Office based on the recitation of the psalms; there would be time for prayer and meditation, manual work and meals, some of which would have been taken in common. On Sundays the monks would have come together for the Eucharist, for which they prepared by a long vigil through the preceding night. In these respects they had much in common with their European counterparts. But there were rather different provisions as far as living accommodation and lifestyle were concerned. Almost certainly the monks would have lived three or four to a simple hut or else alone, and neither all their meals nor perhaps all the offices would have been held in common in the central church which was just another larger hut (stone buildings for all but the landed gentry were still a thing of the future). A circular enclosing wall that served as a necessary protection against thieves and marauding 'highway' men surrounded these huts and the church.

At this early stage of the development of monasticism in these parts, each community would have had an abbot who was chosen from among them for his holiness and gifts of discernment. The abbot had the spiritual care of the monks and the right ordering of their lives. Each community had its own rules and customs. The monks, distinctively dressed and tonsured according to the Celtic fashion – that is the front of the head shaved from ear to ear – formed the inner core of the settlement. Round them, but still within the circular enclosing wall, were the huts of numerous other people including their families. These were the homes of the craftsmen, builders, stonemasons and others who helped to farm the monastic lands and care for the livestock and the gardens. The gardens also lay within the enclosure, and herbs and other produce for food and medicines would have been grown there. Traces of some of these plants can still be found in present-day graveyards sited on these early monastic settlements. In fact the core community of monks were surrounded by all the kinds of people who go to make up a rural community in its almost total self-sufficiency even today. How much this outer ring of people joined in the worship and rhythm of the monks' life we do not know. It is hardly surprising that in Ireland, in the areas where there were larger clusters of people than on Pen Llŷn, the larger monastic settlements came to be known as monastic cities. These were often also centres of learning and schooling for a people, including many of the monks themselves, who were largely illiterate. On the Llŷn Peninsula this was probably true of the monastery at Clynnog Fawr further up along the north coast and founded by St Beuno. St Beuno's monastic activity was widespread even beyond the immediate area as can be seen by the many churches, springs and wells dedicated to him.

The land on which the monks settled was normally given to them by the local lord or landowner, for holiness and holy men were welcomed and respected. This practice of land donation soon led to difficulties and an undermining of the positions of leadership and authority within the Clas. The landowners found their lands being broken up because of their own generosity so that this led, not infrequently, to the landowner himself or one of his sons being 'chosen' as abbot. So a dynasty was formed often with a married abbot, clerical celibacy being optional for priests at this time, though abbots were not necessarily priests in any case. This almost certainly occurred in Aberdaron at quite an early stage in the development of the Clas.

Yet whether these early monks arrived in Pen Llŷn and Aberdaron, singly or already as a group from another monastery, we are still left with the questions of why they came here, what were they seeking and where had they or their forebears learnt of the monastic life? How had they come by the Scriptures? Were many of them literate? Was each group autonomous? There were obviously priests among their number who celebrated the Eucharist. Who had ordained them, trained them, and sent them out? The answers to most of these questions lie buried in undocumented obscurity as far as Aberdaron and Uwchmynydd are concerned. It is only much later that consecutive historical annals began to be kept. Yet there are hints of these very early monastic days and comparison with other better-documented places that allow not unreasonable extrapolation to fill in some of the gaps.

My interest and search was less in the sources and documentation that reflected the political and legal aspects of the Church in these parts than in the spiritual and theological inspiration that underpinned the lives of these early Christians in Wales and especially of those who lived here in Pen Llŷn as monks or hermits. Very early sources, which give an insight into the 'inner' lives and inspiration of these first monks, are scarce if not non-existent in Wales, but Irish sources are more numerous, giving parallel indications of contemporary lifestyles. Welsh oral tradition, however, has been passed down to us through poetry and song and storytelling, set down only later in literary form, so we are not quite devoid of early source material.

The Romans were in Britain from AD 43–410 and they left their mark not only in their ordering of the life of the British people through legislature and taxation, education, military training, road building and agricultural methods, but also through the religions that they brought with them. Most certainly some of them would have been Christians already but also, almost as certainly, they would have found that there were already Christians on these western fringes. Trade routes by sea and contact with Ireland just across the relatively narrow sea-channel that separates that land from Wales would have brought merchants and possibly missionary monks, from the coastal lands of Gaul – that is, the western coastlands of what we now know as France and the Iberian peninsula. Traders from as far as the Near East, following the spice routes through to the Mediterranean and perhaps calling in at the ports of Syria and Egypt, are known to have reached the western shores of Britain. Were there monks schooled in the desert tradition among them? Certainly this was true of Gaul, to whose Christian people Cassian had brought the spiritual riches he had encountered on his sojourn in the Egyptian desert, thus planting a form of monasticism that had not been imbued with Roman-Latin practice and its tendency to regulation and uniformity. My study of Cassian and the early planting of monasticism modelled on the desert tradition occupied me through several long dark winters and must wait until later in this account. But to begin with I was aiming at a broad-brush impression as I had done in my first exploration of the land round Tŷ Pren.

In these early centuries, the promontory that we now know as the Llŷn Peninsula was an important overland route avoiding the dangerous seas around Bardsey with their unpredictable cross-currents. Both the land and sea routes were used, but the alternative of travelling by land cut down some of the dangers and also the length of the journey. Anyone travelling south from, say, Caernarfon to the other side of Cardigan Bay would almost certainly have chosen the safer overland coastal route rather than the waters of the Sound. As early as AD 150, the geographer Ptolemy wrote of this west coast of Britain and mentioned a headland that can be identified with that of Braich-y-Pwll, the headland where I walk often. He also maintained that there were inhabitants of the area who had come over from Ireland, to which the name Llŷn testifies, being derived from an Irish word meaning 'men of the spear'. These men were identified as settlers from Leinster which became Llŷn in early Welsh.

Without doubt the Christian faith was already established in Pen Llŷn by the early part of the post-Roman period, that is, about 440. Two gravestones bearing Latin inscriptions have been discovered here on Anelog in Uwchmynydd, one of which tells of the burial of 'Veracius: priest; and a multitude of brethren', very possibly referring to the existence of a monastic community. The other is of 'Senacus: priest'. These stones are dated to the late fifth or early sixth centuries and both are now in Aberdaron church. A further stone was found at Llannor, a little further north on Pen Llŷn, bearing the Latin name 'Vendistali', known in Welsh as Gwynhoedl. His church and settlement is but a few miles from Aberdaron in what we know as Llangwnadl. This stone is now in Plas Glyn-y-Weddw, an art centre and gallery in Llanbedrog. Four other early gravestones were also discovered in the near vicinity, one uniquely not of a monk or priest, but of a layman: a doctor. This stone stands in the graveyard at Llangian not far from Abersoch on the south coast of Llŷn.

A hazy picture began to emerge for me of the presence of very early monastic settlements in this area, almost certainly closely linked to Ireland and possibly equally closely linked with the Welsh Borders of what is now Powys, and with South Wales. The names of Beuno and Dyfrig bear witness to these links, and even that of Samson. Samson is an illusive character and is best known as Samson of Dol and as a bishop in south Wales. The Samson often mentioned in northwest Wales is unlikely to have been this same Samson as there is no evidence that he came so far north from Caldey Island off the southwest coast of Wales. Someone called Maelrhys is also mentioned and a chapel just north of Aberdaron at Llanfaelrhys still bears his name.

Lleuddad and Hywyn were closely associated both with Bardsey and Aberdaron, and Aberdaron church takes its name from them though little is known about either of these gentlemen other than through much later hagiographies. Little by little, as I read, I began to find indicators of what I was searching for. I also realized that these first monastic settlements were always very small, often only four or five monks and never more than fifteen, after which some would split off to found a new group elsewhere. All these historical details may seem a little irrelevant at first but, to those visiting this area now on their own spiritual quest, they often add to their experience of this *place*, colouring its immediacy and giving it context.

The archaeological, political and legal documentation gave a conceptual historical background but did little to help me in my search for what inspired these early monks. What was their 'inner landscape', in the sense in which we would interpret this today, and why, if at all, did they seek out this rugged, spare coastal region? Was it in part a deliberate choice or was it more an unconscious quest to find an 'outer landscape' that matched the inner, something that the desert monks had certainly sought and found? And another thread closely allied to the outer landscape was that of the question as to whether there was such a thing as *Welsh* Celtic spirituality with an identity of its own that was making itself felt in my own life here so many centuries later in this land so rich in an unique culture. On this level an incomer like myself finds they are living in a foreign land.

Almost certainly, as has already been said, those very first monks came as missionaries, to an area where Christianity had probably never yet penetrated. The landowners, or at least some of them, having an innate respect for a holy man, gave them land on which to settle and establish themselves. Far from seeking out this area as somewhere remote and rugged, a Welsh equivalent of an Egyptian/Syrian desert, they were on the direct route between the coastal districts of mid-Wales and the shipping channels of the Irish Sea. This is in contrast to how things are now when Pen Llŷn seems relatively remote and off the beaten track. Access by road is at a distance from the nearest motorway, and the scenic railway, which meanders along the south coast before veering inland, crawls at a pace essential to preserve the weakened bridges over estuaries and rivers. In those early medieval centuries the peninsula lay along-side what was a shipping 'highway'. Yet quite early on there are signs that, at least in Lent, some of the monks, either in groups or singly, on a more eremitic search, withdrew to some wilder un-inhabited part of Pen Llŷn such as Mynydd Mawr and Anelog in Uwchmynydd, or even across the treacherous Sound to Bardsey. The Island beckoned, standing there close to the horizon, the seem-ing edge of the world, its mountain reaching up towards the heav-ens and therefore closer to God, for this was still a flat three-tiered universe with God above and the underworld of darkness below. The earliest contact between the Island and south Wales is better documented than that between the Island and the much closer mainland of Uwchmynydd, but there is a persistent unverifiable tradition that some monks from Anelog, this side of Aberdaron, began to spend Lent on the Island. So the beginnings of a seeking out of rugged solitary places started to emerge.

The historical landscape changed, as the Pax Romana receded, yet at the same time contact with Rome and central Europe in-creased. So the organized monasticism of, first, the Augustinians from the twelfth century onwards and then the Cistercians – a stricter reformed branch of Benedictine monasticism – began to replace the freer ways of those earlier Celtic monasteries both in Wales and Ireland. Yet the search for solitude, silence and the chal-lenge of the wilderness continued, and hermits came to find some-thing of what they sought in these wilder parts far from the nascent urbanization that had begun to spread into Wales from England, albeit still far from the coasts of this Peninsula.

What sort of life did those early Celtic hermits lead and how did it differ from the more strongly regulated and centralized orders of northern Europe? Where had they learnt that way of life, and who were they? As to who they were, that is perhaps the 'easiest' question. Names such as Dyfrig and Cadfan occur early in records, as 'The Lives of the Saints' began to be written, albeit long after the deaths of those whose lives they described. These hagiographies are much embellished with legendary accounts of spiritual feats and miraculous healings, instantaneous travel from one distant place to another (bilocation), and the gushing forth of springs that were soon identified as holy wells with healing properties. There is the added confusion of persons through variant spellings. Even so it is well documented that Dyfrig had been ordained by Samson in about 521 – Samson being a bishop in south Wales and there-fore able to ordain priests. He was also someone who had trav-elled widely in Brittany and Gaul where he had learnt much of the monasticism that Cassian had established after his sojourn in the Egyptian/Syrian deserts among the monks there. Dyfrig himself later also became a bishop but fled to Bardsey seeking solitude and the challenge of this wilderness island. He died on the Island and his grave was later identified and his remains translated to Llandaff in Cardiff. Both Lleuddad and Maelrhys were known to have been disciples of one Cadfan who travelled widely throughout Wales leaving an itinerary of churches named after him from the Gower Peninsula in south Wales to Anglesey. But it fell to Lleuddad and Maelrhys to penetrate Llŷn, and at least the former spent time on Bardsey as a hermit. So these are records which go back to the early part of the sixth century at least, and point to this *place* as being already sought out as a wilderness, inhospitable but challenging for those seeking God in solitude, and not just as an area to be missionized.

Perhaps the best description that I could find of the eremitic life in these parts at this time was in a short book by Mary Chitty.[3] She describes something of the life of Elgar the Hermit, known only from the Book of Llandaff that places Elgar towards the end of the eleventh century. It would seem that the description was written

3 Chitty, M., 1992, *The Monks of Ynys Enlli, Pt 1: c. 500 AD to 1252 AD*, printed privately.

not long after Elgar's death for it is not embellished by what was almost de rigueur for hagiographies of that time, with striking portents and miracles that emphasized the holiness of the saint. This undramatic style gives it a ring of authenticity and some leads as to why he, and others, sought out Bardsey as the place where they were drawn to live. For Elgar it was not so much a chosen place but somewhere that he came to see as a gift from God, a place 'chosen for him'. Elgar was an Englishman from Devon who was kidnapped as a child and taken to Ireland as a slave. He eventually became the property of the king and was forced to act as the royal executioner. This involved killing with his own hands all those who were condemned to death. This must have been a miserable existence in the extreme, from which he somehow managed to escape, only to be shipwrecked on Ynys Enlli. So strictly speaking Elgar did not seek out this rugged island but rather found there that which he was seeking, albeit unwittingly at first.

It seems that for seven years Elgar lived partly alone and partly with the community of monks already on the Island, from whom he learnt much in preparation for his life as a hermit. In this he followed what was common practice dating back to the early desert tradition, of training in the corporate life of a community before receiving the blessing of the abbot and brethren to move to the margins and live as a hermit. For the next seven years he lived entirely alone. 'His was a life holy, glorious, chaste, with very little bread, threadbare clothing and lean of face.' He depended on what he could garner from the sea for food and 'what the angels brought him'. We are not enlightened as to the appearance of these 'angels', but we are told that Elgar revealed to Caradog – another very different hermit from south Wales who undertook an arduous journey in order to spend time with Elgar who was known for his holiness – that he, Elgar, was visited in bodily form by the holy spirits of those who were buried on the Island. Whatever they told him he found to be true at all times. It seems they also told him where to find food, though not every day; also herbs and water. Elgar admitted that he was often hungry, disgusted and suffered from indigestion, which makes one wonder what strange fare he sampled and how very ascetic his life had become. Quite explicitly we are told that he was following this way of life as a penance and as a way of owning responsibility for those he had been forced to kill as royal executioner to the king in Ireland. Caradog tried to persuade Elgar to leave the Island or to come away for a short time. Or if he felt he could do neither of these, to at least modify his lifestyle, but Elgar resolutely refused and 'retired at once to his praying place', having been told by his ghostly guides that he must not leave the Island.

Whether Elgar was literate we do not know, but as was common at that time he will have learnt the psalms by heart and quite probably long passages from the Scriptures. He obviously led a very disciplined life not only of body but also of thought and spirit. He will also have imbibed the tradition of the monks of the Celtic Church and desert spirituality that saw a longing for, and accessibility of, God by his creatures, as natural and strong. This is something which the later medieval Church of the West largely denied, seeing 'the Fall' as a total severing of a natural relationship with God that could only be restored through the gift of grace. To our contemporary minds, Elgar's life was one of extreme asceticism, and yet it also has a balance and a healthiness about it that rings very true to me and links my present pale form of the eremitic life in this place and the twenty-first century with something of what drew Elgar to remain on Bardsey. His ascetic discipline is surely based on the same desire to eschew those things which for *him* would have distracted him from God, leading to greater clarity of thought and intimacy and also a deeper awareness of the world around him in all its beauty and suffering. The actual *place* played a great part in his decision to remain, even though he had not sought it out in the first instance. The fact that he was on an island obviously aided his resolve to remain where he was.

What was this idea of the holy person, of holiness, which was much revered in these early times? What was their vision of 'holiness'? Elgar adds a dimension when he speaks of the spirits of those who had gone before him on the Island as being in a very direct sense his mentors. They had left their 'footprints' on the Island, giving to the *place* something it did not have before. These early monks and hermits having been drawn to this place, had found something 'special' there. By what had they been drawn? For those who followed in their footsteps, the place now held an extra quality through the holiness of those who had gone before; something extra had become part of the rocks and sea, air and land, part of the spirit of the place itself. These many centuries later, this quality remains: a transparency, a threshold quality, where the seeming boundaries between our sense of time and timelessness, are crossed or glimpsed. Those who had lived here in those early times, both on Enlli and also on the mainland of Pen Llŷn, are present to us now not only through the dedication of the churches, wells, springs and the Pilgrim Way itself, but through the 'footprints' they have left on the land itself. Consciously or unconsciously, this quality has become part of the very being of those whose inheritance is both this land and its history, as I found when I came to know some of the local people a little. But I had come to seek God in the solitude, stillness and space that I hoped, in my ignorance and preconceptions, I might find here. What I found were all these but they were essentially bound up in the *place itself.*

Given that the first monks were probably drawn here on a missionary quest, that they were welcomed by the landowners as holy men, given land and encouraged in the Christian faith which they initiated and taught; given that some of them were drawn to the margins of their communal life for times of withdrawal and a deeper spiritual quest; given that gradually the solitary eremitical life began to grow in this remote area perhaps because, paradoxically, it was at that time less remote than now being within reach of sea routes bringing contact with Irish and probably Gallic and Near Eastern Christians and missionary monks; given all of this, what was it that inspired those early monks and hermits in their quest for holiness? Was it a purely personal almost self-centred quest, something that has always been levelled against, and been a snare for, every hermit? Or was it a life that involved 'love of neighbour' in a radical sense? St Anthony's[4] saying sprang continually to my mind: 'Our life and our death is with our neighbour'. Obviously for Anthony the hermit life was rooted in 'love of neighbour'. How could it be otherwise if it flows from the love of God, the heart of God? Yet what did these early Celtic monks and hermits understand by 'holiness'? I began to explore this quest and its recognition in those early days, wondering as I did so whether it is possible to get inside a culture and time so far removed from our own. My touchstone was that lives, the imaginative intuitions and fruits of those lives, whether recorded for us through words in 'stories' or poetry, song or image or more formally, live on, if they have at their heart something of the eternal truth and wisdom, love and compassion which is God.

I have seen the mystery of poetry use the world as wax, in the same way as day illumines the solitudes of night, and night reveals the secrets of day.

Sea trims ridges and pebbles on the beach, a river wears away the rocks on its banks, sand turns with the wind, and clay yields to the rain.

And poetry is the child of the sea and the river's heir, the wind kindling sand in its trail, and the rain softening the clay.

If the world were an unchanging place, we would know no calm in the tumult of the wind, or restlessness in the satisfaction of the rain, and poetry's sleep would be a sleep without dreams, and her waking hours sightless, for dreams work on wax, visions on clay, and they give poetry's shape to the river's solitudes and its form to the secrets of the sea.

---

4 See *Athanasius: The Life of Antony*, 1980, trans. Robert C. Gregg, SPCK. St Anthony of Egypt (c. 250–355) is thought to have been the first hermit-monk.

Day and night are wax, with stars melting everywhere, falling and stopping on the branches of a tree that had previously been an empty sieve, and forming a pattern of snowdrops and primroses where turf had been barren so long.

River and sea are wax, running to their end in the night, and re-formed without end with the coming of the day.

Sand and clay are wax, like a desert turned into a blossoming whirlwind, like soft earth showing the mark of boots.

I have seen night turned into day, so that night could not remain as before, seen a river become a sea, and there was no need to be worried, in spite of some unexpected turn of events, that the flood might stop, and again I have seen the sands of the seasons settling as grassy dunes in beds of clay.

Ovid had seen sea that had become land, he had seen anchors on the tops of mountains.

Such are the acquisitions of poetry, all things retained, all things changed, the preservation of a love that re-fashions the wax of day and night, the river's wax and the sea's, the wax of sand and clay.[5]

---

5 Bowen, Euros, 1993, 'Metamorphosis', in *Euros Bowen: Priest-Poet*, ed. C. and S. Davies, Church in Wales Publications, p. 29.

Six

Desert Spirituality and the Quest for Holiness

It is winter. The days are short and increasingly cold. The nights are long and there is an added sense of darkness over the earth and sea. But it is not a brooding darkness, rather one of change of vitality, of tempo, of thrust. The new growth and greenness of spring, the cycle of new lambs and calves, of fledgling birds and burgeoning wildlife, the blossoming of summer, of migration, the ripening of fruits and the seeds of autumn, all this is over. Land and sea lie 'dormant'. To a large extent living creatures go about their business of survival only. The fortunate few hibernate. Only the storms, gales and occasional brilliant days of sunshine give colour to the sense of illusiveness, the seeming sleep of winter. For me the winter brings a change of rhythm also. Earlier to bed, I get up a little later for the dark hours before dawn, as pivotal in winter as in summer, stretch well into what would be the light of a summer's day. When the wind drops the enveloping darkness is so still that the lighthouse beam, silhouetting the Island beyond the Sound, throws mysterious silent shadows over a sleeping world. I sit and wait, drawing my being back from its wanderings again and again as attentiveness is withheld or given.

During the short hours of daylight the rhythm is different too. In the depths of winter the ground is too wet or too hard for gardening; rather it is a time for harvesting winter vegetables and checking on stakes and battens and making sure the birds have water when the rare frosts are severe. So I walk more in the winter though never straying too far afield.

Winter is also a time for poring over seed catalogues and beginning to plan the garden for the following year. This is not an easy patch on which to grow vegetables or flowers for the salt-laden winds blowing straight off the sea burn the leaves of almost all plants and dry them until they are left crisp and brown and almost useless either for nourishing the plant or me. It has taken me several years to begin to know what will flourish and what varieties can stand the harsh conditions better than others. A cold frame made from discarded windows and breezeblocks is proving invaluable, as is windbreak fencing.

One dark November morning, after days and days of rain and grey skies, once more wearily I pulled on waterproofs, wellingtons, scarf, gloves and hat and waded through inches of mud across the fields. Coming to the gate in the field above Tŷ Pren, I was just about to open it when the dripping bush of blackthorn by the latch burst into flame scattering a riot of bright yellow sparks into the leaden sky. In a flash all was transformed. From the depths of the shelter of the bush a knot of yellowhammers erupted, dispelling the gloom and drizzly rain in an instant of glory.

Praying sitting on a rock or cliff top is also rare in winter though there are days of almost warm sunshine. But I eschew any attempt at repetitive words of prayer while walking or working out of doors, though some find this helpful. Even after years of praxis, learning to do just one thing at a time does not come easily. 'When you are walking just walk; when you are digging just dig; whatever you are intent on give it your whole attention. Whatever you are doing, do it with the whole of your being and as though it were the only thing to do and as though there was all the time in the world', a counsel of perfection given me by Bishop John V. Taylor at the very beginning of my solitary exploration, echoing the wisdom of countless others all down the centuries. Rarely can this be even a remote possibility in most women's lives. For me it is and, in a sense, carries a double responsibility: to practise this single-pointedness not only to deepen my own attentiveness but also on behalf of others caught up in unrelenting multitasking. Life and the work in hand is the prayer or, put the other way about, the prayer is the work. We live in a world characterized by extreme activism, restlessness and rush, yet a hallmark of this solitary life needs to be *otium*.

> The woods are lovely, dark and deep,
> But I have promises to keep,
> And miles to go before I sleep,
> And miles to go before I sleep.[1]

Ah, the many 'promises' with which daily life lures me away from the practice of *otium*. No time, no time – rush on! But why? To what end? Time and the passing of time have such a hold on us.

Winter is also a season for more reading and writing, going to greater depth into the themes central to the main thrust of my life. As I write mainly in the winter months so I realize how great a part the elements play in my life and so in shaping what I write. Each winter has its own uniqueness yet also underlines the essential rhythmic repetitiveness in a solitary's life, honing the skills which enable stillness at heart's centre to begin to emerge.

In winter also, crafts largely take the place of gardening and are as creative as coaxing new life from the soil. One day while in Aberdaron, I had walked along the deserted beach and collected some of the exquisite pebbles. When I got home I experimented with various Celtic designs of knotwork and interlacing patterns using a black pen. Drawn in waterproof black ink on the smooth stones the designs came out well and I realized also that these pebbles fitted snugly into the palm of my hand. Lying in my open hand their weight and design were an aid to centring my busy mind. I gave them away occasionally to a seeker who had found out my whereabouts or as a thank you to someone who had helped me. To my surprise these pebbles were much appreciated and soon became a part of the crafts through which I could contribute to my

---

1 Frost, Robert, 1943. 'Stopping by Woods on a Snowy Evening', in *Collected Poems*, Jonathan Cape, p. 275.

upkeep until I actually became self-sufficient in covering all my daily expenses.

In the long grey days of winter it is also harder to find ways of laughter-inducing recreation, of breaking the tendency towards intensity, the breeding ground of exhaustion and strain for the hermit. So my reading is more varied. I found biographies and autobiographies together with the best of the classical and new fiction were especially good for their graphic insights into the human condition. The radio too gives the occasional opportunity of interest, music and laughter. But I find I need to watch how much I listen to the radio, for sound, the human voice and even music can clutter my life and mind and play on the emotions more subtly than the written word or material possessions, fracturing the possibility of attentive stillness. Music particularly touches the emotions deeply. But above all I needed to laugh at myself.

And then there is the cold. A cabin with only a thin layer of insulation in walls and roof takes up the temperature of the outside in less than no time if I have inadequate heating. So I pile on the layers and soon resemble the old advertisement for Michelin tyres.

My reading takes me deeper into the background of the history that lies behind the coming of those early monks to this place, this place with its own Welsh equivalent to the fierce landscape and allurement of the Egyptian and Syrian deserts. Gradually a hesitant picture emerged. Having ascertained that almost certainly the earliest monks who came here whether by land or by sea, whether from other monastic settlements in Wales or Ireland or directly from Gaul, with its well-established links with the Egyptian and Syrian deserts,[2] were welcomed as 'holy men', I wondered what was the expectation of holiness?[3] As for the monks themselves, how

---

2 There is a fascinating reference in the Book of Oengus (Irish bishop AD 799), to seven Egyptian or Coptic monks in Disirt Uilaig, an unidentified place in Ireland possibly on the western fringe. The seven monks were included in certain Litanies/Martyrologies of the Saints. (See also Dalrymple, William, 1992, *From the Holy Mountain*, HarperCollins, p. 419.)

3 I owe much of the underlying thoughts of this section to Burton-Christie,

did they see their quest for holiness? Was this similar to that of those first Desert Fathers and Mothers or do the great differences in culture, race and embedded pre-Christian religious customs give hints of more local cultural trends? Do these relate directly to the Celtic roots of this western seaboard of Wales and possibly Ireland?

Egypt in the late first and early second centuries was an area on which the influence of a long Greek, followed by a Roman occupation had left a strong legacy. Prior to the conversion of the first Christians there was a variety of pagan gods, not only the 'indigenous' ones of the local religions, but also those from Greek, Roman and Judaic/Semitic cults. These all existed side by side without undue friction and without the missionary aspect towards conversion which characterizes Christianity. Inherent in the beliefs of followers of Isis and Osiris was the hope of resurrection, which may have been a small contributory factor in the comparative ease with which Christianity was embraced in parts of Egypt from the second century onwards. It is thought that many of those who were educated and literate among the first Christians were probably Greek speaking and Greek educated, an education grounded in the philosophical schools of the Stoics, neo-Pythagoreans and Neoplatonists. I am not well grounded in philosophy so have to take this on trust. There were also widespread Greek and Persian ascetical religious movements such as the Gnostics[4] and the Manichees[5] and ancient Judaic ascetical movements such as the Essenes.[6] There may even have been distant influences of Buddhism, given the trade routes from the Far East through Egypt to the Mediterranean. All this led

---

Douglas, 1993, *Quest for Holiness: The Word in the Desert*, Oxford University Press.

4 Gnostics: characterized by a belief in intuitive spiritual knowledge of revealed religion.

5 Manichees: held religious beliefs based on the supposed primordial conflict between light and darkness, goodness and evil.

6 Essenes: ascetic Jewish sect that flourished in Palestine in the first centuries BC and AD.

to an interesting seedbed for Christianity and accounted, in part at least, for the springing up of apparently heterodox Christian belief systems. It was not until the Seven Ecumenical Church Councils, beginning with that held in Nicaea in 325, that an 'orthodox' or unified Christian belief system was defined and refined. This, then, was the background to the early Christian monastic movements that grew up almost simultaneously in Mesopotamia, Egypt and Syria, Cappadocia and on the continent of Europe.

It soon became evident that for these early Christians as opposed to the adherents to Late Antiquity philosophies, the quest for holiness followed a different path. This quest for both pagans and Christians was regarded as coextensive with life itself, with the universal search for 'God', which was something pursued by so many at that time. Spiritual purity was also a common aim, but its interpretation and how it could best be attained was, perhaps, the main point at which the two quests took their different paths. For both pagans and Christians it was an *individual* quest focusing 'holiness' for the masses in the 'holy man', who was revered for just this reason and on whom they modelled themselves as 'disciples'. The pagan holy man was a philosopher, a lover of wisdom in the ancient Classical sense. Pagan wisdom was based on the ability to think and act through the knowledge, understanding and experience of a particular school of philosophy. The Christian holy man, monk or *monachus*, took the characteristics of his life from the root meaning of that word: sole or single, undivided, attaining an inner unity, free from care, all of which was marked by a high degree of renunciation and ultimately a celibate lifestyle. A key text was the Gospel saying of Jesus: 'If you would be perfect, go, sell your possessions, and give the money to the poor, and you will have treasure in heaven; then come, follow me' (Matt. 19.21).

The pagan philosopher was a learned and often also prosperous man who lived at the centre of society. The pagan schools of philosophy flourished in the urban centres of the world of Late Antiquity. They taught a philosophy of life that was rooted in society and was for the transformation of that society through a simple lifestyle. The pagan 'holy man' sought to transform *himself* through the power of his reason. By contrast the Christian monk, or 'holy man', withdrew to the margins of society, to a place of deliberate marginality, in which through attentiveness to the Holy Spirit's promptings in his life he might learn to discern the way of transformation. This was God's doing and not something he could do through the power of his own will and reason alone.

The monk's life was counter-cultural and influenced by a strong sense that the radical teachings of the Gospels and 'example' of Jesus, Son of Man, were becoming more and more eroded, especially for Christians living in the cities. This began as early as the second and third centuries. Yet also all through these first centuries the Roman rulers who administered the land often persecuted Christians for their refusal to worship the emperor, so their lives were hardly easy. With the conversion of the Emperor Constantine in AD 311, the persecution of Christians largely ceased and Christianity became widely adopted as a 'state' religion. This greatly accelerated the erosion of truly Christian values and practice in the eyes of many Christians. So these early monks withdrew to the margins of society, to the desert, away from the prosperity of urban life but therefore also away from centres of learning.

The desert was a naturally fearful place and proved to be one that imposed its own asceticism, which became integral to the monks' very survival. As they began to develop a way of life in these new surroundings, so even for those among them who were literate there seemed to grow a certain disdain for learning and for what they saw as 'secular philosophies of life' (a trend not altogether alien among some Christians even now, in the twenty-first century). The hermit-monk, through his withdrawal from society and his withdrawal even from his fellow monks, worked out *within himself* the tensions and temptations that are faced by all men and women living together in society. These were his 'demons' that lay *within himself* and called out for transformation and ultimately transfiguration. In more contemporary language, we might say: integration and transformation of the universal human instincts and desires. The word 'demon' conjures up all sorts of images in our contemporary minds of little red devils with hooves and horns and whiplash tails. The way of life developed by these first desert monks appealed not only to the literate and prosperous, but also to the unlettered poor, opening up for them a life in which they had a certain autonomy and self-esteem that was denied to them in urban society under the Romans. Society at the time was strictly structured according to rank and attributes and those with none of these had little status. But there was also another reason for the flight to the desert, which was to avoid heavy taxation and possible conscription into the vast Roman army and almost certain exile.

Did withdrawal to the desert and the adoption of a different lifestyle alter the concept of the Christian 'holy man'? Originally the quest for holiness by the masses was focused on example and teaching, on the lifestyle and personality of the 'holy man'. Was this still a strong thread in the desert or did withdrawal from all but minimal contact with other people cloud the monk's sense of his shared humanity and focus the quest almost exclusively on his own personal holiness? For Anthony, the first documented desert hermit, solidarity with his fellow human beings certainly remained paramount. Working out within himself the temptations that are part of all our lives, one of his best-known 'Sayings' sounds a clarion note of authenticity which warrants repetition in this narrative: 'Our life and our death is with our neighbour'. Athanasius, who visited Anthony in the desert, wrote a *Life of Anthony* which had a great impact, bringing the 'desert' to the attention of those in authority in the Church and placing its traditions right at the centre of the development of Christian spirituality. The words of Athanasius (296–373) carried authority as he was Bishop of Alexandria from 328, and Alexandria was one of the greatest centres of learning at that time.

Anthony saw that it is 'with our neighbour', in our own inner thoughts about others, let alone when we are actually with others, that the authenticity of our lives is seen in its true light. How strongly and colourfully I increasingly found this to be true, as my busy mind roamed and responded to the presence of those with whom I had contact through memories, letters and occasional face-to-face meetings, and the ever-present temptation to judgemental-ism, which is of a very different quality from discernment.

For those steeped in a classical education the monastic quest necessitated replacing the philosophical ground texts by the Scriptures, which involved, in a very real sense, a transformation of basic assumptions. Yet they were still the educated people that they had been, and so they continued to use the tools of interpretation that they already knew. But now their interpretation of the Scriptures was coloured by their radical lifestyles, giving rise to the stories and 'Sayings' that we now attribute to them, which are as vivid to us now as they must have been to their disciples. It is only through this rich record of 'Sayings' and stories that we know of their lives in such detail. Those who visited them came away with a sense that they had sat at the feet of holy men and were fired to disseminate what they had witnessed. It is through the writings of Athanasius and Cassian and many others that we owe so much of our knowledge of the desert or eremitic tradition.

With the conversion of Constantine and the freeing from persecution, Christians became more zealous in their work of evangelization and the making of converts. Society needed to be christianized, as they truly believed that this offered the only road to salvation. So alongside the monastic ideal of the holy monk or hermit who *withdrew* to the margins of society, there developed the 'holy man' who re-entered society after many years of exercising extreme renunciation and ascetic training.[7] His re-entry into the 'market place' was greeted with awe. He was credited with possessing supernatural powers and was called on to minister to troubled consciences and give advice, and his prayers were considered to be highly efficacious. He was also regarded as being imbued with gifts of healing,

---

7 I owe much of the thought behind this section to Brown, Peter, 1971, 'The Rise and Function of the Holy Man in Late Antiquity', in *Journal of Roman Studies*, 61, pp. 80–101.

the power to avert natural disasters, to foresee the future and to ease social tensions. This image of the 'holy man' was of someone at the heart of society, someone whose function was above all *social*. He was called on to mediate and even arbitrate and to provide protection for the vulnerable. The monk or hermit who remained in the desert was also sometimes involved with those who came to consult him, and the same supernatural powers were assigned to him, as we know from many of the Sayings of the Desert Fathers. But for them the points of direct contact with others came through men and women seeking them out on the margins – they did not throw open the doors of their monasteries and hermitages. Both these images of the Christian 'holy man' in Late Antiquity see him as a key point of intersection between the spiritual, wider cultural, social and even political forces of the time. Whether he was alive or had died, he was reverenced. The movement of return to the centres of society was centripetal; the flight to the desert was centrifugal, yet at heart they had much in common: the good of their 'neighbour'.

Though twenty-first-century society, especially in the West, is so different, there are parallels. We also live in an age in which the Church is much exercised with the 'christianization' of a largely non-Christian/post-Christian and multicultural society, but perhaps the 'Idea of the Holy' is not one much considered. And yet – and yet – drawing out to the margins into solitude and learning to live in however small a way 'at the point of intersection where the love of God and the tensions and sufferings we inflict on one another, meet and are held to God's transforming': does not this hold echoes of the lives of those early desert hermits? Are there not echoes here of a centrifugal lifestyle in a largely activist centripetal Church yet with 'love of neighbour' still at its heart?

Did this desert tradition of Late Antiquity spread? The newness of this monastic life lay in its locus and the questions this threw up. The Scriptures, especially the teachings and life of Jesus the Christ, the Man, indicated a way of life and praxis which was not a theoretical philosophical system to which the intellect alone assented, but a life-giving inspiration directly from God, in God and with God. A picture emerges which remains clearly recognizable in the rise of early monasticism in Gaul and Brittany, Ireland, Scotland and Wales: the Celtic fringe of Western Europe. Something similar was also emerging in the heartlands of continental Europe through the advent of Benedict (480–550) and his monastic foundations, but though this latter monastic movement began at much the same time, its inception within the Roman culture of Italy laid foundations that reflected at least in part this different soil. The Romans were very legalistically minded and so a *regulated* life under a strict monastic Rule and rules encouraged a different underlying ethos from that of the monastic life that grew from the roots of a freer Celtic people.

With the advent of the Romans into Wales, travel by land as well as sea had opened up a little more – in the north the Romans penetrated well into what is now Gwynedd, though possibly not far into Pen Llŷn and Ceredigion. The Roman soldiers were under the command of relatively educated Roman citizens, some of whom took up residence with their wives and families especially in south Wales. For them Latin was their lingua franca and their educational inheritance. So Latin infiltrated the western Celtic fringe of Wales not only through the missionary monks from Gaul and Brittany but also through the invading Romans, some of whom were already Christians and had brought their Christian faith with them. As the Romans withdrew, so the more western continental Christianity that they had brought with them declined, having had but a tenuous hold within this 'Celtic' culture. This left a vacuum eagerly filled by those first Celtic monks.

Two names – among others – stand out as being of great influence in the planting and growth of early monasticism in the Celtic fringe which gave it its distinctive 'ethos' as opposed to the more systematized early monasticism of 'Roman' Europe. The two are Martin of Tours (335–397), and John Cassian (360–435) who came from Marseilles. Both men were highly influential in their ministry in Gaul. Both, independently, had visited the Egyptian desert, where they spent time living and conversing with the monks and hermits. What they had undoubtedly heard about, they became eager to experience for themselves and to learn what it was that inspired these lives of prayer and worship, discipline and work. Returning to their native Gaul, they independently laid the foundations of an indigenous monasticism based on a similar vision. Parts of Gaul were deserts of sorts, barren scrubland, but in the main the fiercest landscapes were in the mountainous areas and along the rugged exposed stretches of the coast open to the prevailing winds and storms off the Atlantic. These 'desert' regions remained unurbanized, unlike Tours and Marseilles that were cities of size and seats of learning. So, as in Egypt, this early monastic movement took root on the margins of society, attracting some literate men – whose education would have been more Latin than Greek – but also those who were illiterate and who were probably in the majority. Both Martin of Tours and John Cassian wrote about the inspiration they had found in the desert but it was John Cassian's works, especially the *Conferences* and *Institutes*, that became widely available (and were also prescribed reading for the followers of Benedict). That monks from Gaul found their way not only to Brittany but also to Ireland, Wales and Scotland, is undisputed, as is the traffic in the opposite direction. The trade links by sea were well established and copies of many parts of the Old Testament and the Gospels as well as the Psalms, were probably first introduced in this way – as well as through the Roman invaders during the Pax Romana.

Latin rather than Greek – and obviously not the vernacular – would have been the language of the first copies of the Gospels, Psalms and parts of the Old Testament brought into Wales. At the same time, it seems likely that knowledge of, if not copies of, John Cassian's *Conferences* and *Institutes*, which formed the basis of the monastic movement he and Martin of Tours inspired in Gaul, were also known on this western fringe of Wales. The earliest manuscripts of monastic rules, liturgical texts, homilies and prayers that survive are deeply indebted to these early monastic texts. But they were being planted in this very different soil, and the teachings and words very soon took on the distinctive spirit of the bardic tribal traditions embedded in the culture of the Welsh peoples. This was no uniform planting of a loosely systematized set of rules and customs, but rather the embracing of a way of life from within an existing, vibrant culture. Wales, Scotland and Ireland all developed their distinctive variations.

Though there appear to be no extant manuscripts of which sources of scriptural texts were available to the earliest monks in Wales, the writings of St Patrick (390–461) in Ireland are peppered with many biblical quotations whose sources can be traced, which indicate that there were many links with influential figures in continental Europe as well as the Celtic fringe of Gaul and possibly the Egyptian desert. It does not seem far-fetched to extrapolate from Ireland to Wales. Patrick's use of the Psalms showed that his source was a Gallic manuscript, possibly that of Hilary of Poitiers. Quotations from the Old Testament and the Book of Revelation predate Jerome's Vulgate of 334 – which was regarded as the first authoritative translation of a large part of the Scriptures from Greek into Latin – while the Acts of the Apostles is pure Vulgate. The Gospels were a mixture of Vulgate and pre-Vulgate, again using a Gallic text. It is thought that Patrick may have had direct access to these manuscripts. It is known that he originally came from the northwest of Britain, possibly Cumbria, and though he was captured and taken over to Ireland as a slave, he managed to escape back to Britain and may have been educated at Whithorn in Scotland where there was a good library, before returning to Ireland as a missionary. It was some time before I realized the importance of tracing the sources of the Scriptures which were used by the first Celtic Christians. Their origin gives a good picture of how the desert tradition reached this Celtic fringe.

This early monasticism found fertile soil in which to grow. The fifth century was a time of great activity and interaction between influential figures within 'Christendom' and the nascent Christian monasticism of the desert tradition. Wales was involved in an aspect of this interaction in an unsought for way. Pelagius, whose British name was Morgan, indicating that he almost certainly originated from Wales, travelled to Rome where he exerted a substantial influence especially among the aristocracy. His aim was to establish a *perfect* Christian Church as an example to the sinful world. He claimed that human beings could achieve perfection by their own powers through their use of free will. This ran counter to Augustine's teaching. Augustine taught that *all* depended on grace. Augustine's influence as Bishop of Hippo was great compared to that of this 'upstart' Pelagius. Pelagius saw 'original sin' as no more than Adam's bad example and not as an inherited defect which impaired the freedom of the will. The determined opposition of Augustine saw the Pelagian heresy condemned by two successive Church Councils and by Pope Innocent I. But Pelagius was a Briton and that is possibly partly why Pelagianism appears to have become embedded in early Celtic Christianity and monasticism with its emphasis on the inherent goodness of creation and an unbroken relationship with the Creator as well as its close affinity with the natural world and the soil.

But the Celts were realistic and did not misread the human condition and our tendency towards self-centred actions that separate us both from God and from our fellow human beings. Penitence played an important part in the life of the Christian Celt, counteracting any tendency towards unbridled Pelagianism. However, so strong was the condemnation of Pelagianism that Pope Celestine I sent Germanus – who certainly travelled through Wales – to advise the bishops of Britain in 429, and Palladius to be Bishop of Ireland in 431, thus strengthening the links with central figures in the Church of mainland Europe. But there may have been another reason for the strongly held sense of the inherent goodness of creation in early Celtic monasticism. This may have come through the writings of Irenaeus (130–200) who was Bishop of Lyons from 178. With the links that were being increasingly forged across Christendom it is more than likely that some of the writings of Irenaeus and others of the early Fathers of the Church had reached the western fringes of Britain. Irenaeus wrote that 'the glory of God is a man

fully alive.' What could be more affirming of the essential goodness of our humanity?

Apart from Patrick, the fifth and early sixth centuries also saw such
great figures as Ninian – in Scotland – and Gildas, who wrote from the
Welsh context and deplored the withdrawal of the Romans, Finian
in Ireland, and Illtyd and David in the south of Wales. It could be
said that Finian together with Gildas laid the foundations of the Celtic
monastic culture. In the fifth century also, perhaps as a result of the
belief held in mainland European Christianity that sin after baptism
was thought impossible, the Celtic Church with its more realistic
outlook was inspired to write what were entitled 'Penitentials'. These
were manuals that linked ascetical ideals with down-to-earth pastoral
realism before setting out a list of penances for various sins committed after baptism, thus making room for forgiveness as something
that could be repeated. Monks in particular are mentioned in some
of these Penitentials – and there seems to have been no sin that wasn't
described in graphic detail – so that these manuals became an integral
part of Celtic monastic practice. Also seemingly unique to Celtic monasticism was the concept of three types of martyrdom. Athanasius'
Life of Anthony had shown how central the theme of martyrdom was
to Anthony. Celtic monasticism spelt this out in three distinct ways:
white, green (or blue) and red martyrdom. Martyrdom here is used in
its root meaning of 'witnessing'.

> The white martyrdom for someone is when they part for the
> sake of God from everything that they love, although they may
> suffer fasting and hard work thereby.
>
> The blue martyrdom is when through fasting and hard work
> they control their desires or struggle in penance and repentance.
>
> The red martyrdom is when they endure a cross or destruc-
> tion for Christ's sake, as happened to the Apostles.[8]

---

8 Davies, Oliver, 1999, 'The Cambrai Homily', in *Celtic Spirituality*, The
Classics of Western Spirituality, Paulist Press, p. 370.

Many threads came together for me as I steeped myself in these early traditions. There are as many ways of living a solitary life as there are solitaries, but for me the roots of the eremitic tradition were basic and ones that I found I was intuitively drawn to and was adapting to the twenty/twenty-first centuries.

Seven

Grey – the Colour of Hope

It is winter once more. The storms and gales have been raging with scarcely a lull since mid-November and it is now the end of January. All this week there have been dire warnings on the shipping and weather forecasts: violent storms are sweeping in from the Atlantic from the southwest. The first land directly in their path is this headland and peninsula. I check that all is secure and stow away anything still movable in the garden. I have found by bitter experience how gale force winds can pick up and send quite heavy objects hurtling into the air dangerously close to the windows. I inspect the ridge tiles of the cabin and the corners of the roof. All is as safe as I can make it and I come back indoors as it grows dark, hoping against hope that the forecasts are exaggerated. So far the wind is high, high enough to deposit thick layers of rime on the windows, making them sparkle in the rare moments of sunshine that had punctuated the day, but that is not unusual. As I prepare for bed I know I shall find it difficult to sleep, as I shall have one ear cocked as the noise of this battering storm rises to an uneven crescendo.

Eventually I drift into a troubled sleep but almost immediately, or so it seems, I wake with a start as a huge clap of thunder shakes the cabin, followed by an uneasy lull and silence. Then sheet after sheet of lightening fills the room as though there were no walls or curtains and broad daylight had forced its way into the night. It feels like the very early hours yet it is still only shortly after midnight as the storm announces itself, rumbling its furious approach. Then the first gusts gather force, whipping straight up from the cliff. Gust follows gust each one stronger than the one before, the on-slaught broken only by fleeting moments of eerie silence as though the elements are drawing breath. No sooner has the cabin collected itself, than it is hit once more, bucking like a frail barque on a heaving sea, and my bed shudders under me. I lie still, every sense alert, stretched into the wildness tossing the world around me as though we were nothing more than the plaything of some wayward fiend. The noise is deafening.

All night long the tempest raged. I got up wearily and no sooner had I put on the light than it flickered uncertainly and went out, leaving me not only in the dark but also in the cold. I was now connected to mains electricity and even boasted one small storage heater, having proved to the community's satisfaction that I had found my feet here and could face into the challenges . . . My usual reasonably even spirits plummeted. Dejectedly I got out the emergency camping lantern, Calor-gas heater and small gas ring that I have for just this sort of emergency, and made a hot drink. All day and into the following night the storm raged and the overhead power lines remained down, presumably over a wide area of the peninsula. No repair crews could possibly risk life and limb while the hurricane lasted, for it was now given out as a hurricane of Force 12 strength. The news, when I switched on the transistor radio, told me almost triumphantly that the strongest winds recorded so far throughout these islands were in Aberdaron – 94 mph gusts – which meant that on this exposed headland they were even in excess of that. The weather station that relays wind speeds and all the other data necessary for the safety of our coastal waters is only a quarter of a mile from Tŷ Pren so I knew that the media, who always love a good story, were not exaggerating the reports.

The radio might have been an anchor for my thoughts through all the tumult around me, but the roar and noise of the storm was such that even at full volume the words were almost drowned out. Dismally I sat it out, wrapped in a rug for warmth but unable to settle to anything even during the hours of daylight. Obviously I could not go out or even think of opening the door. Would this frail cabin survive? Once before, in a previous hurricane, the corner of the roof had blown off with a huge cracking wrench that had signalled danger in such menacing tones I had had to vacate the cabin and stagger, half crawling, across the fields to the farm where they gave me shelter. That time a lull in the storm had eventually made it safe for a builder to reach us to secure the remaining roof at least temporarily. The poor man had to rope his ladder to the cabin to keep it in place and himself to the ladder. Even then he had found it difficult to balance or to keep his mind on the job, unable to believe his eyes. The sea – not just spray – was washing right over the headland some 100m high. This was the same builder who had made Tŷ Pren habitable when I first moved in and had since also insulated the walls and roof in an attempt to keep some of the little heat that I had from escaping. He knew all the idiosyncrasies of the cabin and took pride in keeping it ship-shape. His family had lived in the area for generations but never in his lifetime could he remember quite such a sustained hurricane.

As I sat huddled in a rug my imagination began to run riot and to range over the world, pushing out beyond the boundaries of the scene which was playing itself out all around me. War raged in Iraq and Afghanistan. In Africa the conflicts, famines, illness and the epidemic of HIV/AIDS had spread their tentacles to the Indian subcontinent and out into Indonesia and beyond. Global warming threatened to change the face of the earth irreversibly through our profligacy and the thinning of the ozone layer. Though connected with the wider world, what was this local storm in comparison with disasters on that scale? The more I tried to pray the darker and heavier my spirit grew. The 'still-centre' was wracked by conflict, let alone by the noise and tumult. Somehow the hours passed and the storm blew itself out. After another 24 hours the power lines too were restored. But my spirits did not rise.

Time passed and each day and night were a struggle; I felt as though I was wading through thick sticky mud giving way occasionally to quicksand which threatened to pull me right down into the bowels of the earth. I tried every strategy and vehicle of faith and common sense that had served me well at times of despondency or crisis in the past, for despondency, or *accidie*, is a well-known visitor to those living a contemplative life. Naturally it is especially difficult for anyone living on their own. In the corporate life of a community the regular call to worship holds each one within the whole. If we are on our own we do not have this support yet we *are* all, as it were, like knots in a net that connects us to each other as members of the human race. If one knot breaks the others hold the net together until the rent is mended or strengthened. Each time when I had had periods of enveloping greyness before, they had proved, in retrospect, to have been opportunities for a new beginning or even a strengthening experience. But now? Could I go on? Even: would this small cabin continue to stand if this winter was the harbinger of a permanent change in weather patterns? It was of little comfort to have been told by Gwilym the builder that Tŷ Pren was unlikely to collapse around me but rather that the roof would blow off first.

Day followed night, night day. I stuck to the bare minimum of my life's rhythm, setting my face like a flint to remain 'in the cell'. I took two or three days 'off' yet remained anchored in the cabin. Nothing changed. Winter gave way to spring and then to summer and autumn. Still my inner landscape remained unremittingly grey. It had been a warm and sunny summer, enhancing the beauty of this place, but nothing seemed to penetrate that heavy shroud under which I cowered. If anything the beauty, which I barely noticed through my unseeing eyes, added to my low spirits. My inner being was splintered and also at odds with the outer; the thresholds were barred.

What sort of an attempt at a life of 'loving and unceasing prayer' was this as I added my greyness to the downward spiral of an increasingly pessimistic world and merged my inner voice with those of the prophets of doom? Hope is not the same as optimism, but what had happened to hope, let alone faith? Did I believe at all; love at all? What did I mean by 'faith'? Yes, I knew it in my head as 'the assurance of things hoped for, the conviction of things not seen' (Heb. 11.1). As best I could, I continued to live as though I 'believed' as this was the only way of remaining on course; 'things hoped for', yes, but 'assurance'? I felt none in my heart and my head was of no help either.

There are so many facets to daily life, yet each is integral to the whole. At heart's centre I am scattered and my thoughts and my imagination threatened to run unchecked down alleys of fantasy and dissipation listening to the voices urging me to give up. Their reasoning was cogent: it was my pride that was keeping me here and it was time that I realized that I was not strong enough for this life either physically, psychologically or spiritually. I was never tempted to spiritualize what was happening to me or to label it grandly as a 'dark night of the senses and soul' so minutely described by St John of the Cross. The many facets of life were imprisoning me within a crystal that reflected the light outwards before it could reach me. It seems as though this life had become a vehicle of destruction, adding to the ills of the world. Yet even as the 'demons' spoke I knew that it was fear that was underpinning the wretchedness and vaunting itself as pride in every guise, or even as prudence, and as false masks of a splintering self-knowledge. Almost at the limit of my spiritual and physical tolerance, I stopped struggling at last.

Where had I been? Gradually, very gradually the pall lifted and I woke one morning as the dawn was breaking, and once more my ears heard the birds singing as the sunlight reached the top of Enlli mountain and crept down to reach the sea below as the world woke to a new day. Almost a year has passed.

> Thou mastering me
> God! Giver of breath and bread;
> World's strand, sway of the sea;
> Lord of living and dead;
> Thou hast bound bones and veins in me, fastened me flesh,
> And after it almost unmade, what with dread,

Thy doing: and dost thou touch me afresh?
Over again I feel thy finger and find thee.[1]

I begin to pick up my reading again and move from the Eastern
deserts more firmly to this Celtic fringe of Wales as I realized my
study of the eremitic tradition threatened to become too abstract
and conceptual. The culture of the peoples who inhabited the
western seaboard of Wales had little in common with that of Egypt
or Syria. In the early centuries of the first millennium this western fringe would have been a cold and largely tree-clad land apart
from a narrow coastal strip and the hilly areas where exposure to
the storms and lack of soil depth precluded growth of anything
beyond scrub and rough grassland. The population was scattered
and sparse, a tribal people with local dynasties. There were few
if any conurbations and, before the coming of the Romans, education was centred only among the relatively well-to-do ruling
families. Even there it would have been fairly rudimentary and
probably mainly, if not exclusively, in the vernacular of the district
though a little Latin might have been included. The history of the
people was preserved and recorded, handed down and embellished
through a vibrant tradition of poetry and ballad, song and music.
This is a very different background to that of the early Desert Fathers. Here there were no schools of philosophy – the Druidic cult
is hardly comparable – rather this was a rich culture marked by a
closeness to the *land* and the everyday experience of the frailty of
human survival. This was an agrarian people who claimed the land
not only as their inheritance but as their very livelihood. Belief was
expressed through praise of God for the natural world and its inherent goodness and fertility, fear of its power to destroy if abused,
and thankfulness for its gifts to maintain life; a continual offering
up of praise and calling down of blessings. For the common people, survival was the dictating principle. This was no philosophy

1 Hopkins, G. M., 1948, 'The Wreck of the Deutschland', in *Poems*, 3rd
edn, Oxford University Press, p. 55.

of life, worked out and written down, but a living culture whose uniqueness was recorded through their poetry and song embedded in the land and the relationship between the people and the land.

As we have seen, Latin, rarely Greek — and obviously not the vernacular — would have been the language of the first copies of the Gospels, Psalms and parts of the Old Testament brought into the country. Similarly copies of John Cassian's *Conferences* and *Institutes* would have been in Latin. The earliest manuscripts of monastic rules, liturgical texts, homilies and prayers that survive are deeply indebted to these early monastic texts. But they were being planted in this very different soil and the teachings and words very soon take on the distinctive spirit of the Bardic traditions embedded in the culture of the people. This was no uniform planting of a systematized set of rules and customs but rather the embracing of a way of life from within an existing, vibrant culture.

The movement to the margins from the cities, which underlay the beginnings of desert monasticism, had its equivalence here in detachment from the tribe and the family group and so also from the life-sustaining inheritance and ownership of a specific area of land. This meant a severe loss of both security and status, as land given to the monks by the lords of the manor was given to the group or monastery and not to an individual monk. Nor were 'Sayings' a natural form of expression in this culture, but rather poetry, stories and song both in Latin — among the more literate monks — and the vernacular. The tradition was passed on not only through the written word but possibly primarily, orally, incorporating elements of pre-Christian pagan beliefs within the telling. Among these is the strong tradition of the holy man as being someone possessed of power not only to heal but also to curse. *The Life of Beuno* brings out this distinctly Welsh Celtic flavour in stories of curses with fatal consequences giving the opportunity also for miraculous outcomes. There is the well-known tale of the beheading of Gwenfrewi – Winifred – by the spurned King Caradog whom she refused to marry. Not only was she restored to life but a spring with healing properties sprang up where the blood from her severed head had soaked the ground, healing not only people but also animals, another intrinsically traditional trait. *The Life of David* speaks more of his asceticism and care of the sick and needy than of quasi-magical power, but both saints are closely associated with healing wells and springs and *places* made holy by their having preached or lived there. But these *Lives* were written long after the deaths of those they commemorated and read as though there were many added embellishments.

In the written texts of early medieval Ireland and Wales, in addition to liturgical material there is a rich vein of devotional prayers including 'litanies' and 'loricae', meaning 'breastplates' – as in 'St Patrick's Breastplate' known to many of us in its modern form as a hymn. A breastplate was something that was buckled on over the heart where it served as a protection. These prayers were intended essentially for private use, to consecrate the whole of life as a gift from God, night and day, work and food, and all the minutiae that go to make up life in all its aspects. There are prayers for the blessing of the hearth, the milking of the cow, hoeing the soil, prayers before and after meals, birth and dying, and always on waking and before lying down to sleep. Protection was especially petitioned for the hours of darkness. All these prayers were intended for frequent repetition to give spiritual and temporal strengthening.

In more specifically monastic devotional prayers there is a marked emphasis on an asceticism that furthers holiness of body, mind and spirit, spelling this out in detailed 'Penitentials'. Asceticism was seen above all as a means to an end, not an end in itself. God and God alone was the goal and his own 'reward'. It was not thought that we are rewarded for our good behaviour or good deeds, as these are just part and parcel of the Christian life. Asceticism was much admired as a mark of holiness and the quest for holiness, but this in no way contradicted the paramount belief in the basic goodness of human beings and all creation. Yet even in these written Penitentials there is no single template, no single monastic rule, but rather local rules set by local abbots and monks.

Poetry took up many of the themes of devotional prayers especially of praise. There are some delightful examples by hermit monks rejoicing in the details of the natural world, of land and seasons, wildlife and birdsong. But also as in later texts of the desert tradition, hagiographies abound, as do homilies, some interpretation of the Scriptures and some theological texts.

It is from Iona that we have perhaps the earliest fragment of a poem from a Celtic monastery: a praise poem composed on the death of Colum Cille — Columba — and possibly dating from as early as 550. In this fragment both Basil — one of the founders of monasticism in the East — and Cassian are specifically named as monastic teachers.

> He applied the judgements of Basil
> who forbids acts of boasting by great hosts.
> He ran the course which runs past hatred to right action.
> The teacher wove the Word.
> By his wisdom he made the glosses clear,
> he fixed the psalms,
> he made known the books of Law,
> those books Cassian loved.
> He won battles with gluttony. . .[2]

In conjunction with my reading about the history and development of Celtic Christian monasticism, I continued to feed my life on the desert tradition and its development. As the monastic life of the deserts of Egypt and Syria became established, so more permanent settlements sprang up, with hermitages at some distance from those living corporately in order to ensure a greater solitude and silence. These early monasteries were probably just clusters of adjacent caves in the rock face of the mountains, with those of the hermits more scattered and at some distance. Only gradu-

---

2 Dunn, Marilyn, 2000, 'The Amra', in *The Emergence of Monasticism: From the Desert Fathers to the Early Middle Ages*, Blackwell, p. 145.

ally might a larger simple building or cave be used by a group
of monks for the corporate saying of the Office and the celebration of the Eucharist. Some of the earliest Christian paintings
have been found in these monastic caves and simple churches.
There was no ban in the Christian tradition (as there is in Judaic
law), on representations of holy people in paintings and images
or of holy scenes and symbols. The majority of the monks were
illiterate but depictions of the stories and people within those
stories would have brought instant recognition. Though they
were not literate, they were able to 'read' these paintings, these
images. Standing before such an image was an invitation to cross
a threshold, to enter into the new transfigured world of God's
gift through Christ. The earliest images were almost certainly
of Christ himself, the Face of God in Christ, the very image of
God. Image/Icon: the same word is used in the narrative of the
creation when God says, 'Let us make man in our own *image*'
(Gen. 1.26).

These painted images were the precursors of what we now know
as the Icons of the Eastern Orthodox Church with their distinctively traditional and highly systematized forms of representation.
An icon painter 'writes' an icon. It is a work of prayer in which
he is not expressing his own insights through his artistic gifts but
rather he is 'writing' an image through which we approach as it
were a threshold. This is part of worship, of a liturgical tradition
of invocation and praise, an invitation to prayer. Icons help us to
cross the threshold between time and eternity in *both* of which
we already live and breathe. Icons have become popular among
many Christians who are not members of the Eastern Orthodox
Church and used by them as a great aid to devotion. Gradually
recurrent themes are found among these icons, recalling not only
biblical stories and biblical people, but also images of the holy men
who had laid the foundations of the desert tradition, particularly
Anthony and Paul of Thebes. Freestanding sculptures in stone
would not have stood up to the fierce winds and storms – sandstone is too soft – but bas-relief did feature in later years.

In Wales the early monastic and eremitical tradition developed within its own cultural setting and gradually became more familiar to me. I recognized, through my identification of a shared *place* in which I had now lived for many years, the life about which I was reading. The footsteps of those early saints and hermits had left an imprint on the land. Their spirit and the inheritance of their 'holiness' imbued the very rocks, let alone the people. This heritage, which had attracted but little attention for centuries, was now, in the twentieth century, being explored and researched with great interest. There was a renewed interest in the *places* in which we have our roots, not just in a nationalistic spirit but also in a way which lays claim to the past as part of the present, permeating the boundaries of time and space and our understanding of our history and ourselves.

I found that alongside the solitary life of the hermit in Wales in particular, there was also a tradition of the *peregrinati,* whose emphasis on marginality and leaving of kith and kin involved having not even a cave or hut as the bounds of their life but having *nowhere* permanent to lay their heads. They had no monastery or home of their own to which to return but carried their stability within themselves, living it out literally, wandering from place to place.

As monasticism became established so also solitude began to be sought more often as a prerequisite for greater austerity and silence in a life given primarily to prayer and praise. For this a remote and fierce landscape, swept by the elements, was seen as the essential setting, the 'desert' of Celtic Wales. Here too, in this culture so unlike that of the Egyptian desert, oral transmission and the written word were not the only vehicles of communicating the faith and monastic practice. Wales, too, had its 'icons'.

The visual art of early medieval Wales traces as close an affinity with Gaul, and via Gaul with the Egyptian and Syrian deserts, as do the manuscripts of the Scriptures, the Lives and Sayings of the Desert Fathers and the *Conferences* of John Cassian. By the ninth century monastic houses would have had some small-format manuscripts of the Gospels and Psalms used most probably for personal devotion and study, though very few solitary hermits would have had their own. But there were also larger illuminated Gospel books for ceremonial and liturgical use and display. These manuscripts are a written history in themselves, the origin of each recognizable by the unique differences in scripts and styles and illumination. By the early ninth century there are marginal notes in Welsh hands in the vernacular as well as Latin. But it is in the artefacts written in stone that we find some uniquely Welsh 'icons'. There was no shortage of stone in this rocky mountainous terrain.

The earliest stone artefacts known to us date back to possibly the first half of the fifth century: the grave slabs found in Uwchmynydd itself are among the earliest. This is a harsh but temperate climate with a soil depth that, though shallow, did allow for the interment of the dead and made possible the incising of marker stones to commemorate the sacred places of burial, a practice not possible in the Near Eastern deserts. Some of these burial sites, regarded as holy because of the people who had lived and died there, soon became places of pilgrimage, often with churches named after the holy man who was revered as a local saint. The periods from which these grave-markers originate can be distinguished by the changes in the incising of the lettering. Until the end of the sixth century Ogham uncials – a script used principally in Ireland – show the close sea link between Wales and Ireland. Roman capitals occur through the period of the Pax Romana, AD 43–410. Grave markers are often incised with what we recognize as universal Celtic art forms as used in the decoration of the Celtic manuscripts of the Scriptures and other texts: knotwork, intricate interlacing patterns, animal and human representations and figures from the Scriptures or of local saints and bishops. For later generations they provide a rich historical record of the development of monasticism in these early centuries.

However, the simple standing stones and rough-hewn crosses were only the precursors of an iconography that could be said to reflect something equivalent to the *teaching* value of Eastern icons. The great High Crosses of the tenth and eleventh centuries, often incised with the typical Celtic 'patterning', also carried scenes from the Scriptures, of the historical faith or of local saints. These magnificent carved crosses are a Celtic form of imagery/iconography 'told' in stone. Of great interest are the frequent representations that referred to the beginnings of monasticism and the desert tradition. There were scenes depicting Anthony, the first monk and hermit, together with Paul of Thebes – another early hermit – and also Basil the Great, who was regarded as the 'founder' of the corporate monastic life in the East. Locally, at Penmon Priory on Anglesey, a tenth/eleventh-century cross records the temptations of Anthony. In Scotland, a seventh-century Pictish stone from St Vigean's, near Dundee, illustrates a scene from the Life of Paul the Hermit showing Anthony's first meeting with Paul.[3] They are shown in profile, which is in itself unusual, seated in high-backed chairs facing one another. Each has one hand outstretched to hold a round loaf of bread. The story has it that as each one deferred to the other they could not agree on who should break the loaf, so both pulled together, each taking what remained in his hand. But the significance of this unusual depiction of the two saints is its origin in an early Coptic icon. The original icon is lost but the scene is recorded in the side panel of a much later seventeenth- or eighteenth-century icon of a conventional rendering of St Anthony. Here, in the side panel of a largely unremarkable icon, are Anthony and Paul in Paul's cave, sitting facing one another with outstretched hands grasping a round loaf with a line drawn down its centre! How did this scene reach Pictish Scotland as early as the seventh century? Paul and Anthony also occur frequently on Irish High Crosses and there is another magnificent example on the Ruthwell Cross in Scotland. These artefacts, together with written and oral texts, show indisputably the communication between the Egyptian desert, Gaul and Brittany and the Insular Celtic lands, one with the other.

A picture emerged, for me, of early medieval monasticism on this western fringe of Wales and the search for solitude which drew those

---

3 Dalrymple, Williams 1998, *From the Holy Mountain*, Flamingo, p. 420.

first hermits to its westernmost coasts bordering the Irish sea. The search for solitude was also a search for a *place* that matched their inner being and need to do battle with their demons in a radical following of the Gospels. As for those first desert hermits, so for these first Welsh Celtic hermits, the working out *within themselves* of the tensions and temptations that are common to us all was the basis of their calling and quest for holiness. The culture and ambience was very different but essentially the quest was the same. This rings as true to me now in the twenty-first century as it did then.

> Every cell in our bodies
> knows how to die;
> only minds have to learn
> to let go
> to dance in the spiral
> or drift to the ground
> and wait to be stirred.[4]

The winter seemed extra long and severe this year. It is March, yet the first signs of spring seem to have stalled. Each day the strong north wind blows unrelentingly, cutting right through me as I struggle across the fields to collect milk and post from the outbuildings of the farm. The snowdrops in my garden have come and gone. The first primroses, surprised by earlier sun and warmth, have been burnt by the salt-laden winds and look a sorry sight, shrivelled and brown. Only the celandine survive and at the first intimation of sun, open their tightly closed buds and greet the world with a defiant glow of gold. Each night the wind drops, the clouds part and the intense cold deepens into a frost so keen that, as I draw back the curtains, I see a world transfixed into immobility, stiff and stark yet incredibly beautiful. My windows are deco-

4 Evans, Christine, 1989, *Cometary Phases*, Seren Books, Poetry Wales Press Ltd, p. 103.

rated with intricate ice-flowers such as I have not seen since the war when there was no fuel to bring heat to a bedroom. Not even the novitiate floor at the convent had been as cold as this though it is true that we did sometimes have to break the ice on our morning washing water. Occasionally the wind veers slightly into the north-west and it becomes a tad warmer – even one or two degrees can make themselves felt. A glimpse of the sun lifts the spirit, and the lambs venture out from the shelter of the hedges and the warmth of their mothers' woolly protection, to play 'king of the castle' and leap all four feet in the air as only lambs can do. Then once again, I wake to renewed frosts and north or even northeast gales threaten-ing snow.

As I write it is beginning to sleet, gradually turning to gentle snowflakes. Within minutes all is transformed. The familiar out-line of headland and Island lose their definition and the sharp rocks and treacherous paths disappear before my eyes, covered now in a deceptively soft blanket. But the snow does not lie for long. The strong winds whip it from the rocks and it soon becomes too cold to snow. We are into our third week of these arctic conditions and if I had come for the *fierceness* of this landscape then this winter is certainly providing it.

This morning I woke to silence. No wind, no sleet, but once again ice-flowers patterning the inside of the bedroom window. Half expecting all to be white and under a blanket of snow, I was surprised to find a heavy frost, but also the promise of sunshine as the dawn broke in a clear sky. A good walk had been impos-sible for the last weeks so I set out later in the morning with an energy I had not felt for many a long day and took the road up the headland. The ground was rock hard under my feet but in the ruts cut deep by the tractor the puddles lay shattered into sharp shards of splintered ice. I climbed steadily using the rough road that winds its way to the top of Mynydd Mawr and the coastguard station.

The gorse and heather, frosted and glinting in the sunlight, shone with myriad rainbows. For an instant I felt like a giant in

Gulliver's Travels looking down on the canopy of a dense forest. As I climbed higher, so the wind began to catch at my face, stingingly cold, and I wrapped my scarf around my head more tightly leaving only a slit for my eyes. The last lap was a struggle until I reached the shelter of the low wall that protects the coastguard hut from the southwest gales – the most usual wind direction. Crouched down on the leeward side of the wall I immediately felt the warmth of the sun and the miraculous calm of a seemingly *warm* March day. The ground was frozen so hard that I stripped off one layer and sat on that in the warmth, my back against the wall, marvelling as so often at the unexpectedness of this place, in which, from one moment to the next a natural threshold is crossed, holding within itself another dimension.

The Sound below me churned with the tide-race in full spate, depth upon depth of icy water. I could almost feel its chill as I sat high up on my cliff top. Beyond the Sound lay the Island, guarded by the sea, its rocky mountain heavy and dark. Nothing stirred, only the winking of the lighthouse on the far tip of the Island. All round me grass and sparse vegetation lay stiff and grey and lifeless, sucked dry by the winds. The soil itself seemed dead. But as I sat I heard the tiniest of sounds: a faint cracking or crackling, the earth itself, touched by the first warmth of the sun, was stretching and coming to life and I could *hear* it. Not long after, a sandy-brown fly with furry body landed on my boot, and then a tiny black ant ventured out of a crack in the soil, until the spot where I sat, which just minutes before had seemed dead, lifeless and listless in its winter drabness, was welcoming the warmth and unclenching the hold of the frost. Relaxed and free, I stayed until the cold had penetrated my inadequate 'cushion'.

The wind had begun to drop so I ventured to the highest point where the whole of Pen Llŷn stretches away to the horizon, the coast of Cardigan Bay curving round to Pembrokeshire in the south, and over to the west beyond the Island, the east coast of Ireland where the Wicklow Hills break the skyline. Further along still lies Anglesey off the coast of northwest Gwynedd with Snowdonia rising range upon range to the northeast. I held my breath, for on each mountain range from Snowdonia down the length of the Cambrian range to the Preseli Mountains in the south and round again to the Wicklow Hills of Ireland, the peaks rose white into the clear blue sky.

Eight

Coincidence of Opposites

Still winter refuses to release its hold this year. The weather patterns are undoubtedly changing, each season less easily distinguishable. I search my memory and cannot remember a March and April in which one day is so cold with a biting north wind that I recoil as I open the door, my hope to begin in earnest on the garden frustrated, yet the next day dawns blue and clear and by mid-morning the sun is warm and I find a cliff-top rock for prayer. Life has become so closely bound to the natural rhythms of this place for me that my body, mind and spirit feel out of joint, shocked by the sudden changes in temperature and mood. The plants and vegetation, birds and small mammals seem equally disorientated, encouraged first by an earlier and earlier spring only to be thrown back into winter after tender new growth has already put out shoots. Even nest building had begun. The effect on the creatures is not as abrupt and confusing as the eclipse had been, confined as it was within the space of minutes rather than weeks, but the sense of confusion is as palpable. Global warming has occurred before and is well documented but was it as swift or is the human factor this time so intrinsic that the spirit is involved on a level other than the 'naturally' observable events? I do not know. Every partial rational answer throws up a dozen more questions as I sit on my rock and gaze out over sea and Island. Gradually my mind's activity becomes a stream flowing alongside the search for silent stillness. The emptiness holds the sense of deep sadness at the seeming disintegration of the earth within the totality of the universe; of the suffering fear of powerlessness of so many and the power-driven fear of the few; of land and sea and air sucked dry and polluted, a crying which only the stillness can hold within the fragile beauty of the day.

An American Orthodox bishop used a poignant juxtaposition of words which resonates with the knots in my heart: *bright sadness*. I look down at the sea below me and suddenly the colour of the water breaks up into its constituent parts like an artist's palette for this water. As suddenly as the spectrum flashed, so the colours re-formed and once again the sea, in normal guise, lapped the rocks below me.

As I walk home along the cliffs mist is rolling in from the north and soon the clarity of only half an hour ago is lost in this new softening of a reality, of a beauty that is too hard to bear for long. Later that night as I lay awake, reliving that extraordinary metamorphosis of the water at my feet, and the almost unbearable coincidence of the beauty all around me within the seeming disintegration and ugly pollution of so much of our world and life, I remembered this thought from a fifteenth-century writer. I remembered Nicholas of Cusa (1401–64), who wrote in his main work *De Docta Ignorantia* that God is the *coincidentia oppositorum*, the coincidence of opposites. 'In God all distinctions are contained and transcended in an ultimate truth, whereas in the world we are unfolding in diversity what is enfolded in the oneness of God.'

In a different way, those early monks and hermits who had come to northwest Wales and gradually sought out these remoter parts of the Llŷn Peninsula had also encountered this sense of *bright sadness*, but for them it was experienced as an opposition from unknown forces. In a seemingly dualistic sense they interpreted these as a direct attack by the 'devil' on themselves and their lives. But for them there were additional sources of 'attack' also. The inner warfare of their personal lives and of the tensions and 'demons' of our shared human condition were not infrequently invaded from outside also by brigands and blackguards, and in a very much more menacing way by the Vikings. In the tenth century in particular, the Norse/Viking raids were frequent and devastating. Monastic sites yielded much sought after treasure, as the churches were being enriched and embellished by gifts of silver and gold chalices and other artefacts of singular value. Yet it was not only, or even primarily, treasure that the raiders were after but slaves. Monks were often fit young men, unarmed and able-bodied, a sitting target for raiders after human contraband. Having pillaged the monasteries the raiders frequently set fire to them, so destroying any manuscripts, texts and books which held no value for them. May this account in part for the paucity of the texts and books of this early period remaining extant in Wales? By the eleventh century the Norse raids gave way to a certain extent to the danger of Irish insurgents and later to even greater dangers from the English from over the border, especially the highly organized Normans.

Yet time and again the monks returned to their monasteries. Had *this place* begun to have a meaning for them beyond the wish to return to their home and place of prayer and work? *This* was where God had led them and no pagan or foreign Christian foe would oust them from planting the gospel and the Celtic-nuanced Christianity in *this* place. They believed passionately that God had led them to *this* place and that he was on their side. At this point in the history of the Welsh Celtic fringe the monastic life was still reasonably vibrant, and the quest for holiness continued to be revered and valued. But as we have said, both the monasteries and the Christian settlements round them had always been small and so their continuance was precarious.

By the twelfth century there are quite a number of reliable written records both of the monastic life and from the princely courts. The church and monastic Clas at Aberdaron was well established, as was a small community, possibly round a monastic church, on Enlli. That Aberdaron and Enlli were interconnected is without doubt and the connection was enhanced as landownership, farming and the development of the estates led to a hierarchy of tasks undertaken by the Clas and centralized in or near Aberdaron. As we have seen, Cwrt in Uwchmynydd – now a farmhouse still of the same name – was the administrative centre for both Aberdaron and Enlli and Secar was the financial office – Cwrt meaning 'court', and Secar 'exchequer'. These are all pointers towards an ever-increasing multiplicity of tasks undertaken by the core community, leading to greater complexity of lifestyle and the inevitable consequence of the adoption of methods to amass wealth and prestige. These aims have never sat easily with the primary thrust of the monastic life and its pursuance of simplicity, if not actual poverty, as a basic precept. The practical weakness of the Clas, as we have seen, was that the holding of monastic and ecclesiastical office and of land and property had become not only heritable but therefore also 'secularized'. There was a fundamental conflict of authority and aim.

Gradually this erosion of the life led to decline. Yet as late as 1188 when Gerald of Wales travelled the length and breadth of the land with Archbishop Baldwin to raise funds for the Third Crusade, he was able to write that:

> Beyond Llŷn there is a small island occupied by some extremely devout monks, called Coelibes or Colidei.[1] Either because of its pure air, which comes across the sea from Ireland, or through some miracle occasioned by the merits of the holy men who live there, the island has this peculiarity, that no one dies there except in extreme old age, for disease is almost unheard of. In fact, no one dies there unless he is very old indeed. In Welsh the place is called Ynys Enlli and in the Saxon tongue Bardsey Island. The bodies of a vast number of holy men are buried there, or so they say, among them that of Deiniol, Bishop of Bangor.[2]

Do some of these extant records point towards a deliberate seeking of greater solitude, silence and austerity on the Island in a way that

---

1 'Colidei' is a word probably derived from the Irish, meaning 'servants of God' which was later Anglicized into 'Culdees'.

2 Gerald of Wales, 1978, *The Journey through Wales*, Book II Ch. 6, in *The Journey through Wales and The Description of Wales*, trans. Lewis Thorpe, Penguin Classics, pp. 183–4.

parallels the flight to the desert? The first monks had come as missionaries. Later a few sought greater solitude and silence especially in Lent, but the monks Gerald of Wales is describing lived in a well-established monastery where others joined them deliberately and probably for life. We are not speaking about a large number of monks but of a small group living an austere and holy life largely uncorrupted by the 'secular' values of the age.

The Welsh princes held the reins of power over the local churches and monasteries for they controlled the purse strings. Yet at the same time, it was the clergy and some of the monks who were often the more educated sector of the local community and therefore through their greater knowledge and expertise linked the princely courts to their lands and so to the income from the land. As the Clas system declined so the landowners saw a very real threat to their power and wealth. If the churches slipped into the control of hands other than their own, especially into the non-monastic arms of the Church, the already insidious struggle for authority would pass right out of their control.

This was a time of reform throughout the Western Church and particularly within monasticism. This reform came from the heart of continental Christianity – Rome – and was disseminated throughout western Christendom. The strongest influence in Wales was the coming of the Cistercian monks, a reformed and strict observant branch of Benedictines, and also the Augustinians. In Gwynedd, it was the Augustinian Canons who took over three of the ancient monastic houses of Penmon on Anglesey, Beddgelert in Snowdonia and Enlli. The Canons were ordained priests who could live 'in the world' though still under the discipline of the Order, or else they could live a corporate life in community. These communities varied greatly in their lifestyles from strict contemplative enclosure to being actively engaged in the Church and among the people around them. The emphasis was changing and was becoming less conducive to an eremitic lifestyle.

Once again I was drawn into pondering our contemporary climate and my eremitic life within it. I find it both comparable and markedly different. Solitude as a lifelong commitment is an anachronism and counter-culture and I sometimes feel like an 'island' in the midst of an increasingly activist Church and world. This is accentuated by the urgency of the global situation and ecological challenges. I know within my own heart how seeds of individualism and self-interest could so easily insinuate themselves. Fear at many levels is polarizing values and beliefs and encouraging the seemingly clear-cut safety of fundamentalism among both believers and atheists. There must be few who are not affected in some way or another. 'Remain in your cell and your cell will teach you all'; the call to faithfulness is like the tide-race of the Sound even when this is invisible as it runs on below the surface of a deceptively calm sea.

In this time of monastic reform in medieval Wales the corporate life in community was also changing. Gone were the separate huts clustered round a central church and surrounded by the houses of the artisans and their families, the pattern that had made up the looser-knit Celtic monastic Clas. An Augustinian monastery would almost certainly have been organized according to a centrally approved pattern where the monks slept in dormitories, worship in the monastic church was in choir – as is still the case in our secularized cathedrals today – and the supporting surrounding offices of Abbot, Prior, Bursar, Sacristan and so on, were similarly uniform throughout the whole Order. Architecturally each Augustinian abbey was built on the same pattern. Individuality, difference, was regarded as a reflection of self-expression rather than self-denial – the 'crossing out of I' – in contemporary language: of the ego. This emphasis does not sit easily with the eremitic life and the trust placed in the individual monk to live in the spirit of his monastic vows.

The Clas in Aberdaron did not survive for long. At first Aberdaron passed into the hands of Augustinian Canons, but after a prolonged period of discord between the new Augustinian foundation on Enlli and the mainland foundation a final rift became inevitable. A community of 'Secular Canons', deemed as such as they did not belong to any of the recognized monastic Orders, did not survive for long either. Most of the land and tenure passed to the Augustinian Abbey on Enlli together with its increasingly complex administration, which continued to be based at Cwrt and Secar. Yet, though the tasks were not inconsiderable, it is almost certain that the community of Augustinian Canons on Enlli never numbered more than a very few men.

With the demise of the Clas came also the probable demise of the few hermit-monks in Uwchmynydd, Enlli and on Pen Llŷn. Enlli as a place of pilgrimage continued for some time, as did many of the other ancient holy places and churches. These continued not only as sites of pilgrimage but also of healing and hospitality. They were served by the Augustinian Canons under the auspices of the Abbey on Enlli. Yet the last word must lie with the monks themselves. The transition from the old dispensation to the new may have been relatively slow. The monks of the old dispensation were probably almost to a man, Welshmen. The Augustinian Canons may well have had Englishmen among their number with an inevitable dilution of the distinctive Welsh Celtic tradition. The end of this tradition as a lived reality is not easy to define and to a degree it lived on in the hearts and spirits of those men who were, above all, Celts. But the monasteries were already in decline, with few houses having their full complement of 13 monks and most were down to three.

The intensely local and centrifugal character of Welsh life became increasingly threatened by England and the subjugation of Wales by Edward I at the end of the thirteenth century was bloody and cruel. Though the land was annexed the spirit of the people was not easily extinguished. The religious life of the Church became more and more centralized, first from Canterbury and ultimately from Rome. This allowed for little local variation and idiosyncratic expression, and the earlier blossoming of a tradition that had encompassed both the more 'Romanist' emphasis on ritual and the more 'eremitic' aspect of godly inwardness, *appeared* to die out, though there is still evidence of its continuation as late as the twelfth century. As the English monarchy gradually lost interest in the Welsh Church so the practice of filling diocesan seats and benefices with absentee English bishops and priests became prevalent. The revolt of Owain Glyndwr – 1400–1415 – certainly had great support in this part of Wales and planted the seed of a nascent nationalism among a hitherto feudal people, but it also brought untold suffering in its wake. Both sides followed a 'scorched earth' policy which affected both friend and foe. This was no longer a 'desert' and fierce landscape in the sense of those earlier centuries, nor was it a political climate in which any form of solitude could have been sought or found. The land was ravaged yet the Christianity that had flourished here in its own unique form did not die out completely.

Change in the hearts of the people here would be slow to come, for the Reformation had first to deal the 'final' deathblow to monasticism as a whole in the reign of Henry VIII (1509–1547), and to the spirituality that lay at its heart. In the early sixteenth century the devotion that had kept alive the practice of pilgrimage and the veneration of the saints and their holy shrines had degenerated into something of a folk religion encouraged by a church in need of money. Throughout Europe the granting of indulgences associated with pilgrimages undertaken, devotions performed, prayers said and donations given, flourished. Though foreign to our contemporary British psyches this had a positive side, as it saw a strengthening of local parish life. In Aberdaron, Llangwnnadl and Llanengan, to mention but three local Pen Llŷn villages, the churches were actually enlarged and embellished at this precarious time. But this proved to be a false dawn. The prevailing teaching on sin, hellfire and the wrath of God does not build up a faith of encouragement and ultimate joy. Fear and negativity are strong bedfellows and crush a people under the power of priest and Church, and a Church continually looking over her shoulder at the political power of the Crown. From reliable records we know that the Abbey on Enlli still administered their estates on the mainland, still welcomed pilgrims both to the Island and the inland shrines. It was perhaps at this time that owing to the dangerous sea-crossing to Bardsey, the tradition that 'one pilgrimage to Bardsey equalled three to Rome' had its roots. But it was not to last. The year 1537 saw the complete spoliation of the monastery on Bardsey. All monastic lands and assets passed to the English Crown. On the mainland the Aberdaron rectory and Cwrt were leased to laymen.

> David's spirit is older than his house
> and its design is greater.
> Mightier than death's heavy blow
> is his word among us,
> and Christ's strength through the branches of the Christian,
> for the fervent chants of the family of gentle saints,
> watches still in the heart
> and will always be known as the hope of humankind.
>
> The way, the life will not cease,
> the truth which the soul loves
> and the tree of finest fruit,
> the Husbandman with the easy yoke.
> His husbandry is in the heart
> and He waits on the rim of our yearning,
> enough for a community and enough
> to yoke together the races through the wide world.[3]

These lines, especially perhaps the last three, suggest that there is something comparable between this time of unrest, with the breakdown of a long established tradition embedded in a culture, and our own twenty-first century. The faith and beliefs of the medieval Church that had stood the test of time were being challenged and dismantled. At the time of the Reformation the political scene and the power struggle between the English monarchy and the Bishops of Rome in Britain and Europe was as powerful a threat as was the

---

3 Williams, Waldo, 1997, 'St. David's' in *The Peacemakers*, trans. Tony Conran, Gomer Press, p. 205. (These stanzas are taken from a translation by Dafydd Johnston with minor alterations and notes by Tony Conran.)

infiltration of the 'old' belief systems by the 'new' theological and pietistic movements. Our foundations too are being threatened. For us there is a passing of a culture in which, until relatively recently, faith in God was still more or less the norm. This is a far more radical shift and without precedence in its rapidity.

Here in Wales the introduction of the Prayer Book in English was much resented. But lethargy bred passivity with the resultant collapse of resistance. Fragments of poetry in the Bardic tradition record a heartfelt sadness among the people of the time, but these poetic fragments soon became rare also. Yet pilgrimage and other age-old devotions persisted in remote country areas where the 'new' preaching had not yet penetrated. There is evidence that the original form of the Mass in Latin continued in parts of Gwynedd well into the eighteenth century. With the translation of the Bible into the vernacular – Welsh – in 1588 by William Morgan, and the translation of the Psalter by Edmund Prys, new life was breathed into the faith and there were pockets of flowering. But the eremitic life as it had been understood within the monastic tradition died out. Only the hearts of the people and the small pilgrim churches, with their adjacent healing wells and medicinal herb gardens, kept the spirituality alive. Because this spirit was never extinguished in the hearts of the people it transferred to the chapels also though its articulation in this tradition was rare.

Morgan Llwyd (1619–1659) was one of these rare writers:

Behold your first task is to be still, and to still every sound that is in your heart, to turn out every thought that is in you but the mind of God in you, to be without thinking of anything but God, who is nothing that you can see . . .

But, you say, Is that possible in this world? Go on, do your best in the strength of God, and the Lord will willingly meet you to give you more strength. But if you first look within and listen to the voices in your heart – there are there the sounds of thorny worldly cares, and the sound of carnal sweet desires, and the sound of an old corrupt guilty conscience, and the sound of hard thoughts about God and men, and the sound of some hope from this world, and the sound of some good works that you have done, or some gifts or grace that you have received, or the sound of the news of the kingdom, or the sound of your task outside. And while the sound of one, yes one, of these is in your mind, you cannot hear the eternal Word.

So seek of God (until you obtain) a still *heart* within, a heart careless of everything but God, beyond the memory of the creature, hidden with God, in God's peace, which is beyond understanding (that peace which was before there was a creature or thought) and as you sink into yourself and from thence out of yourself into God your root, through setting the will on God alone, you shall know the eternal Word in time, who knew you and I before time was.[4] (italics mine)

Morgan Llwyd was writing after the Civil War as the minister of a gathered congregation in Wrexham. There is little actual mention in these thoughts of the whole creation and the natural world as integral to the presence of God, but the basic precepts of 'the prayer of the heart' stands undiminished as the Way and the Truth.

The Agrarian Revolution followed by the Industrial Revolution and the coming of mining and heavy industry to Wales was fertile soil for the Methodist/Nonconformist preachers and chapels. Poverty was acute and education at an all time low. The chapel movement spread, bringing new hope to many, including a renewed sense of community. The Circulating Schools and Sunday Schools brought education in the form of literacy and numeracy, as well as instruction in the Christian faith and Christian morality. The hymn singing that accompanied the preaching sprang from the hearts of the Welsh, so long ground into the dust by poverty and subjugation. Gradually, very gradually, first the churches and then the chapels began to look to their historical roots in Wales and so

---

4 Llwyd, Morgan, 1989, *Contemplation: A Welsh Pilgrim's Manual*, ed. Brendan O'Malley, Gomer Press, p. 146.

to the roots of a people themselves. Old traditions were rediscovered and given new clothes that were woven from the thread of the people themselves, now living in a greatly altered environment. Nationalism played a part in this, instilling a pride in the language and the Welsh as a people distinct from the incomer English.

More than a century later, hidden away on a farm in the folds of the Berwyn Mountains in Powys, at Dolwar Fach lived a remarkable young woman. Ann Griffiths (1776–1805) was an ardent Methodist who lived out her short life on this secluded farm, going about the everyday business of which such a life was made but leaving us a legacy of hymns and poetry which mark her out as steeped in the contemplative tradition of Welsh Christianity.

> ... Here for a few years
> the spirit sang on a bone bough
> at eternity's window, the flesh trembling
> at the splendour of a forgiveness
> too impossible to believe in, yet believing.
>
> Are the Amens over? Ann (Gymraeg)[5]
> you have gone now but left us with the question
> that has a child's simplicity and a child's depth:
> Does the one who called to you,
>
> when the tree was green, call us
> also, if with a changed voice,
> now that the leaves have fallen and the boughs
> are of plastic, to the same thing?
>
> . . .
>
> let us put on speed
> to remain still
> through the dark hours
> in which prayer gathers

5 Gymraeg: meaning 'of Wales'.

on the brow like dew,
where at dawn the footprints
of one who invisibly
but so close passed
discover a direction. [6]

I take a break from my reading and musings and am about to muf-
fle myself up to the ears against the cold when I suddenly realize
that the sun is shining, the sky blue broken only by cumulus clouds,
and the wind has dropped. It is a moment to tread in the footsteps
of those elusive forerunners, away from words and meanings and
concepts, and to walk the headland which speaks of their presence
written in grass and stone, in flower and shrub. Slow in coming,
spring has suddenly burst out in full glory. Taking a path across
the fields I dipped down to the cliff's edge and paused. I had never
seen such an exuberance of colours, growth and birds on the wing.
It was as though the long harsh winter could no longer hold back
the new life of a new year. I paused on the cliff's edge and sat on a
rock that was warm to my hand, and gazed around me. First out to
sea over the racing waters of the Sound to the Island ringed with white
as the breeze lapped the water gently against the rocks. High above the
racing water a group of gannets circled, their intensely white plumage
tipped with black, catching the sun. One, then two more, plummeted
out of the sky and struck the water with hardly a splash, to reappear,
fish in beak and a hasty swallow. The gulls were circling, seemingly
more at random, while razorbills and guillemots – beginning to return from their winter migration – skimmed the surface of the waves
in groups and orderly V-formation, some distant destination direct-
ing their path. Nearer to land, the oystercatchers waited patiently at
the water's edge, red legs and bills contrasting sharply with the grey of
the rocks. Two curlew flew over me, white flashing rumps diverting
attention from their long curved bills, which make them so ungainly

---

6 Thomas, R. S., 2001, 'Fugue to Ann Griffiths', in *Collected Poems 1945–
1990*, Phoenix Press, p. 474.

when on land. Alighting on a boggy strip of grassland, their long legs and bills find the uneven ground unbalancing, yet the search for food gives no respite.

I sat above the spectacular cliff which lies below Mynydd Bwchestyn. The choughs were flying in and out of the holes in the cliff where they nest every year, seemingly deaf to the raucous cries of the fulmars higher up on the cliff face billing and spooning in their elaborate courtship dance, while the 'sentinel' fulmar glides to and fro across the inlet, keeping watch. Last year there had been a raven's nest at one end of the cliff and a kestrel's at the other, both untidily lodged on ledges and so well camouflaged that only the white of their guano gave them away. This year I could see no trace of either of them. A pair of buzzards circled above me, mewing. The short-cropped grass shone with pink and purple and deep red milkwort creeping close to the ground. Everywhere I looked, the beauty of this sudden spring day spoke of returning life, of God's indwelling. Reluctantly I climbed the stile for home and surprised the tiniest baby rabbit I had ever seen away from its warren and safety. The path led across the rough grassland above the cliffs and as I rounded a rocky outcrop which serves as a landmark for boats out in the Sound, I dared walk no further. All around me the grass was blue with squills, the tiny bluebells that grow in abundance on our maritime heath, a carpet of blue mist.

> It is beautiful and still;
> the air rarefied
> as the interior of a cathedral
>
> expecting a presence . . .
>
> here a moment, then
> not here, like my belief in God.[7]

---

7 Thomas, R. S., 'Moorland', in *Collected Poems*, p. 513.

I looked over to the Island, across the racing Sound, recalling the many hours I had spent there and my longer visits of a week or more at a time though never longer, for Pen Llŷn is where I belong. Here, and from my cabin, the Island is constantly framed in my window, etched on my mind's eye, dominating my walks and my 'rock-sitting'. My gaze now is drawn beyond the Island to the far western horizon and the world's edge: a threshold which my gaze crossed.

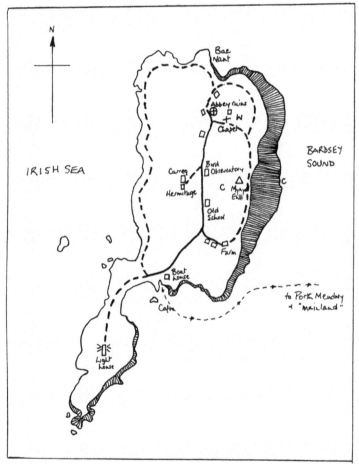

Map 2: Northwest Wales and Bardsey Island

Nine

The Island – Bardsey / Ynys Enlli

We had had storms and severe gales for the past month. The days were rare when the wind dropped and the winter sun showed itself, briefly encouraging the first snowdrops to open to the touch of warmth. One morning I woke to the crying of a lamb. The year was turning and with it came a renewed sense of the wellsprings of life.

The storms had disrupted power supplies three times in a month and during the last long cut in the night, it seemed that Morwenna had slipped while coming down the stairs in the dark and landed on her head on the concrete floor at the bottom. Though the ambulance came quickly to take her to hospital, her condition deteriorated and she died within ten days. The village was shocked, unable to come to terms with what had happened. Morwenna was such a live wire and catalyst in village life. She was caretaker of the school, a linchpin of the church and sailing club, at the centre of the yearly dramatic skit on village life among many other pursuits. And she was just 51; her own mother is only in her seventies, her three girls in their twenties and there are grandchildren too and, of course, Bobbi her husband. Theirs was an old village family spanning many generations. The grief touched many of every age. After over 20 years, I am now part of the community and accepted as such, my living on the margins understood in an unarticulated way – we have a number of mavericks in the area so no doubt I am seen as just another!

This was a funeral it was essential to attend. My kind 'neighbours' at the farm gave me a lift, allowing plenty of time, so we thought. I hardly recognize the family at the farm when they are dressed for a funeral. Wil has a suit that only comes out for funerals and that must date way back with its padded shoulders and wasp waist. The ladies are also demurely dressed in black or dark grey but their frocks seem more up to date.

In the village everything was shut, the shops, the hotels and the cafés as a token of respect which is still quite normal here. Even the school was closed. Groups of young people were congregating and moving towards the church where an amazing scene met our astonished eyes. We were half an hour early but it was already full, every seat taken despite all the extra chairs brought in in anticipation of a crowded service. Packed like sardines, we found standing room only until not another person could be squeezed in and 50 or more stood outside the door on this raw January morning. At least three-quarters of the people were young, in their twenties; all wore black or sombre colours and all were in total silence. There was hardly a sound through all those 30 minutes as we waited, each one wrapped in his or her own thoughts, gaze turned inward, brought abruptly face to face with mortality and the chaos of emotions that so unexpected a death had thrown into sharp relief. Those 30 minutes and the following service, all in Welsh including hymns sung as only the Welsh can sing, showed me that below the surface of a seemingly 'ungodly' generation – in this place at least – lay an innate sense of something more than materialism, consumerism or even the despair which underpins so much of what looks like hedonism. For my own life here, attentiveness and awareness are keywords. Standing in this packed church among a mainly 'unchurched' crowd of people drawn from every generation, attentiveness and awareness were tangible, powerfully focused.

After the service most of us piled back into our cars or else followed on foot to the 'new' church and the family burial plot in the cemetery there. Standing high above the village round the newly dug grave, we looked out over what had to a large extent been the bounds of Morwenna's life. The 'new' church is rarely opened except for funerals. It has a cold unused feel but we had no need to go inside today. The cemetery around it, though also relatively new, felt more welcoming as though already integrated into the life of the village and the surrounding fields through those buried there and their families who visited their loved ones regularly. The 'new' church had been built when in the mid-nineteenth century it was thought that the encroaching sea would engulf the ancient pilgrim church. But the danger receded as sturdy sea defences were built against the tides which now sweep perilously near to St Hywyn's. (Now in the early years of the twenty-first century ominous cracks are already beginning to appear in this new sea-wall.) We stood in silence round the open grave. 'Dust to dust, ashes to ashes' has as sonorous a ring in Welsh as in English as the coffin was lowered into the ground and we paid our last respects to one who in life would never have dreamt that she meant so much to so many. Driving back through the village all was still deserted and for the rest of the day the shops remained closed, as did the school. But for me the lasting impression is steeped in that 30 minutes of sheer silence as we all waited and remembered, each one alone yet all bound together. My thoughts often returned to that silence in the weeks ahead.

Now, once more winter has passed and the sleeping earth has renewed itself. Once more the western horizon beckons as from the edge of the world, as the sea receives the sinking sun setting the water on fire with an intensity of colour only seen in the spring and autumn. Seen from the Island itself this sense of gazing at the edge of the world is stronger still, as the horizon stretches unbroken in an illusory gentle curve, as 'when he drew a circle on the face of the deep' (Prov. 8.27). It is not difficult to enter into the imagination of those in former times, who saw each sunset as the dying of the day and each dawn as the next day's birth, with the sun's rising from the sea once more from the east. My many visits to the Island have imprinted a kaleidoscope of impressions of this on my mind and imagination.

Today I am hoping to cross to the Island for a few hours but the sea is throwing every weapon in its arsenal at us and it will be impossible to land on the shore of the normally sheltered south-facing Cafn, the official landing stage of the Island. If you are not willing to risk life or limb do not cross to the Island by fisherman's dory.[1] Lobster and crab fishing is a serious business, the fisherman's livelihood, and any illicit passenger – for the boats are rarely insured to carry passengers – must fit in with the plans for the day, let alone keep clear of the creels and even the live lobsters with whom you might be expected to share space in the bottom of the boat. Lobsters can move remarkably quickly when in a confined space and have very strong claws. They are also quite beautiful as their richly mottled blue shells glisten in the sun. It is only when they are dropped into boiling water that they turn the lobster-red with which we are familiar on our dinner plates.

So today, if I hope to have some hours on the Island I have to do so via the rocks of Bae Nant, the very rocks that I look out onto every day from the cabin, and by which I judge the direction and force of the wind as the spray dashes against that northern shore. It was at the foot of these rocks that I now found myself. I jumped to safety from the boat and before I could even turn round and contemplate how best to scramble up the boulders, the boat was gone. The thrill of risk steadied me, my sea legs relaxed and my hands and feet found sure crevice after crevice till I stood triumphant on Enlli's centuries-old turf. Immediately the Island took over, and relief and the exaltation of the moment vanished into the wind. I had landed where scores of pilgrims had landed stretching back into the mists of time. Their crossing, unlike mine, would have been in frail skin-covered coracles and would have been truly hazardous, their clothes saturated by sea and rain, their bodies hardened by their long pilgrimage to Aberdaron. Theirs was the end point of a lifetime's pilgrim journey and landfall for them on Bardsey was a moment long anticipated and won only after many

---

1 Dory: the name given to the small motorboat used by the local fishermen.

weeks of real endurance. The ground on which I stood became 'holy ground'.

In the wind and rain I climbed to the spring and well on the mountainside above the monastic abbey ruins and sat for a while gathering together the many threads of the past weeks. Coming so soon after Morwenna's funeral the silence of the Island in winter held a special quality. As always I realized how each visit over the years was different and made for me a chequered pattern woven from threads of a multitude of colours.

This cabin, where I have lived now for many years, stands at the very end of the Pilgrim Way of the Llŷn Peninsula before the crossing to Bardsey. It is Bardsey that the pilgrims set out to reach on their long walk through northwest Wales following the chain of pilgrim churches, holy wells and pilgrim stones set up as waymarks along the route. Here my life is dominated by the Island which stands framed by the window of the cabin. By day I am conscious of its presence wherever I walk, even if at times it is out of sight. By night the lighthouse beam casts a silhouette of its presence, the light swinging through the drawn curtains, making its presence felt as closely as when I draw the curtains back and see its darkened shape against the night sky.

> Grey waters, vast
>   as an area of prayer
> that one enters. Daily
>   over a period of years
> I have let the eye rest on them.
> Was I waiting for something?
>   Nothing
> but that continuous waving
>   that is without meaning
> occurred.
>   Ah, but a rare bird is
> rare. It is when one is not looking,
> at times one is not there
>   that it comes.

You must wear your eyes out,
as others their knees.
    I became the hermit
of the rocks, habited with the wind
and the mist. There were days,
so beautiful the emptiness
it might have filled,
      its absence
was as its presence; not to be told
any more, so single my mind
after its long fast,
        my watching from praying.[2]

I glance up to the wall above the window which frames the Island and that other island stares down at me from beyond the wild coast of Kerry. What is it that makes both these islands on the far western fringes of Wales and Ireland with their deep Celtic roots, such persistent places of pilgrimage? From the fourth or fifth centuries to our present twenty-first century with only a few periods when few were drawn to any form of pilgrimage, their allure has never ceased. Both stand off the northwest shores of the mainland and beyond them stretches the sea to an unbroken horizon. Both are rocks which rise from the sea solidly yet seemingly also precariously, as their smallness is accentuated by the oceans that both threaten and guard them. For the pilgrim living at a time when the earth was flat and the universe three-tiered with the heavens above and the darkness of the underworld below, these two islands beckoned as deserted rugged rocks perched at the world's edge with their summits as close to heaven as it was possible to reach. This was surely part of their allure and over the centuries the holy monks and pilgrims who reached them after much effort

---

2 Thomas, R. S., 2001, 'Sea-Watching', in *Collected Poems 1945–1990*, Phoenix Press, p. 306.

and danger left their footprints on the rock. So a *place* may take on a meaning beyond the *space* which delineates it geographically, a meaning where the natural boundaries posed by sea or land can become thresholds. Here, for some, the veil is stretched gossamer thin at times and eternity is touched from within time.

Bardsey has become as familiar to me over the years as my own more immediate surroundings for it is the fulcrum of this *place and space.* When I say 'as familiar', I make no claim as one who has lived there for extended lengths of time as some have, or as someone who is called to live there. I have never felt this but always that this cabin, Tŷ Pren, on the tip of the mainland, is where I am to be and that it is a 'bridging place'. Both geographically, poised as it is near the cliff top of the mainland peninsula bordering the Sound, and from within my own spiritual being, it is a 'crossing place', a 'bridging place'. We take many paths in the course of our lives as we begin to discern God's leading and the way may become clearer, and often narrows, though for some it can be an opening up, breaking out of the confines of a life lacking any focus or direction. Here in this place, I find that the many paths and different dimensions in which we live our lives sometimes find their confluence, to continue more fully integrated along the unique road that each of us must travel on our life's journey. I write this as a commentary not only on my own experience and through the prayer which has been made here down the centuries, but also from what others have found here and those who may have occasionally found their way to my door. There is nothing special about the door of Tŷ Pren; it is just a symbol of the doorway that is this *place.*

My first visits to the Island were just over the day for a few hours at a time. In those early years I used also to visit the hermit nun who had lived there for many years. Her life was both physically and spiritually demanding. It was no small challenge to brave the long dark and stormy winters alone. On the stormiest days neither the lifeboats nor even the rescue helicopter can reach the Island. At that time also there was no piped water from the hillside well to the houses on the Island, so all the water that she needed she had to carry herself and augment this with large rainwater butts that collected the water off the roof. All this water had to be boiled and filtered. In her small oratory in what had been the old pig-kitchen – where the pigswill used to be boiled up when the adjacent house was still a farm – she had an ancient wood-burning stove. All the wood for this had to be collected over the summer months, mainly from the amazing flotsam and jetsam that was washed up daily by the tides. Each house on the Island had its own pile of wood along the shoreline and woe betide any ignorant summer visitor who raided these piles for a fire on a cold summer's night.

For many months the couple who then farmed the island were the only other people also resident on the Island all the year round, so the winters were truly solitary. I learnt much from her, more through who she was and the transparency of her person than through what she said or even how she lived. Her generation was made of sterner stuff than most of us would claim now and her faith rooted in a more doctrinally orientated Church and monastic setting that no longer holds for many now, so rapid has been the change within our culture. (She was perhaps 20 years older than me.) For her it had been a call to re-establish the eremitic life on the Island that had drawn her after she had had many preparatory years of solitude on the mainland peninsula. Now her footprints too are a part of the legacy of the Island's holy ones. Ever since ill health had made it necessary for her to leave, her hermitage has been in almost constant use by others exploring their call to solitude or prolonged times in silent retreat. They stayed for longer or shorter periods but none have as yet sensed a call 'for life' on the Island. Should this ever become a reality again, it would be to live a different expression of solitude, as the Island is now a far busier place with many more summer and above all day visitors than 10 or 20 years ago.

It was some years before I stayed on the Island for my first week, a relaxed stay taking me out of my solitude for a few days with two close friends. We rented Carreg and had it to ourselves.

We planned it as a silent time, meeting only in the evenings for a shared meal. As I had done when first coming to live in the cabin, I emptied my mind as far as possible of all that I had heard or read about the Island, allowing it to 'speak' to me as free of expectations and preconceptions as possible. I explored the coast with its inlets and rocky coves, sitting for hours with the sea at my feet. Much of the southern and western coastline is made up of millennia-old black basalt rock often encrusted with tiny shells and glistening red sea anemones.

The fields and ancient maritime heath were full of flowers for it was June. The last of the spring was merging into summer so that squills competed with thrift and clover for pride of place. All the tiny creeping wild flowers that were so familiar to me from my headland were opening their blooms to the first warm days of the year. If the terrain round Tŷ Pren is a rich maritime heath land in miniature, the Island is even more so, accentuated by the sea cling-ing so close at every turn. I alternated my walks around the coast with explorations of the 'mountain'. I stumbled on the spring and well – the Holy Well – which supplies fresh water to much of the north end of the Island and lies just above the monastic ruins. The water was icy cold and so clear that the silt in its depths shone with the jewels of thousands of grains of sand and rock. Reaching the ridge and summit of Enlli Mountain I looked instinctively for the tiny grey dot which told me that Tŷ Pren was still standing in the corner of its coastal field. Fleetingly it felt as though I was looking in a mirror that was reflecting my own life back to me. Without realizing it at the time, I was sensing what those first pilgrims who had come to the Island to find their 'place of resur-rection' had felt as they saw the whole of northwest Wales spread out before them, reflecting back to them their past lives. The view from the ridge of the mountain on those clear sun-drenched days took in the whole of Wales from the north coast to the south, from Anglesey to Snowdonia and along the Cambrian mountain range to the tip of Pembrokeshire and St David's Head. To south and west the horizon lay unbroken, until further to the northwest the Wicklow hills and the east coast of Ireland shone uncertainly in the haze.

As I clambered down from the ridge, not sticking to the path, I stumbled on the remains of the hut circles on the mountain slope – not that I would have recognized these grassy mounds as such had I not seen them marked on a map of the Island. On the other side of the mountain narrow sheep paths traversed the steep cliff face of the Island which looks towards the mainland. Perhaps it was foolhardy but I edged my way along the lowest path hoping to be rewarded by entry to the caves at the foot of the cliffs, but it was high tide and these caves are normally only accessible at low tide. It is easier and safer to explore the shoreline by boat. Health and Safety regulations have now closed these lower paths to visitors to the Island, alas. Admittedly there are some risks that are just foolhardy, but without certain risks life can become sanitized and lose a lot of its zest. I returned to sit on the rocky summit, high up on the mountain, away from the other people on the Island – there can be as many as 60 on a summer's day when the day-trips are running – the stillness was intense. It seemed as though I was the only person in the whole wide world, and it was then that I heard the strangest sound as of singing yet unlike any song that I could place. First there was one voice, then another, until it swelled into a choir blending atonally for all the world like singing in tongues.

> Around, around, flew each sweet sound,
> Then darted to the Sun:
> Slowly the sounds came back again,
> Now mixed, now one by one. . . .
>
> And now 'twas like all instruments,
> And like a lonely flute;
> And now it is an angel's song,
> That makes the heavens mute.[3]

---

3 Coleridge, S. T., 2005, *The Rime of the Ancient Mariner*, Enitharmon Press, pp. 205–6.

I glanced down at the Cafn and the rocks in the bay where the seals lay basking in the sun, a veritable choir echoing from rock to rock.

The richness of the bird life with its many visiting migratory birds surrounded me wherever I went. There are hides placed at strategic points along the coast and perched on the rocks on the mountain, for Bardsey is designated as a site of special scientific interest not only for its birds but also for some of the other flora and fauna, and the minerals that make up some of the rocks.

My first night I woke frequently, unused to having the room floodlit by the sweeping beam of the lighthouse. The beam rotates to a set repetitive pattern but this cuts across one's own rhythmic heartbeat and breathing so was, at first, disturbing. Not long after midnight I woke again, this time to a distant eerie calling that grew gradually louder until the night sky was filled by the sound of hundreds of Manx shearwaters flying in under cover of darkness to feed their mates in their nests in the deserted rabbit burrows deep in the bowels of the earth. At present there are no rabbits on the Island, much to the relief of the farmer. A few nights later we ventured out after midnight to where the burrows had seemed particularly densely packed along the banks of the northwest end of the Island. As we waited, again that distant eerie calling began to fill the night and soon answering calls came from the burrows, as though heaven were calling to earth and earth to heaven. Within minutes birds were tumbling from the sky and landing all around our feet completely unafraid. (On another visit when I had taken my sleeping bag up onto the mountaintop to catch the sunrise and must have dozed off, I was woken by a sudden impact from above as a shearwater landed on my chest, as astonished by my presence as I was at its arrival.) These birds, so beautiful in flight or on the sea, are quite ungainly when on land. Unbalanced by their heavy bodies and short-legged webbed feet, they become easy prey for predatory gulls. So it is only on dark nights that they fly in often having to spend many days and nights out at sea waiting for the moon to wane or clouds to gather.

Impression followed impression on that first longer visit. Our stay culminated with a climb to the summit of the mountain in the very early hours to see the sun rise over the mountains of the mainland and the light gradually infusing another day. As my eyes scanned the horizon I chanced to look towards the west and there was the moon sinking into the western sea as the sun rose in the east. I remembered those early pilgrims who had climbed the mountain at *sunset*, it is said, and looked out towards the east over the mainland where their lives lay mapped out with the view over the whole of Wales. Turning away towards the west into the setting sun they died a natural death. For me that early morning, the confluence of sunrise and moonset remains imprinted on my spirit and felt far from being a harbinger of death.

> There is an island there is no going
> to but in a small boat the way
> the saints went, travelling the gallery
> of the frightened faces of
> the long-drowned, munching the gravel
> of its beaches. So I have gone
> up the salt lane ...
>
> There is no time on this island.
> The swinging pendulum of the tide
> has no clock; the events
> are dateless. These people are not
> late or soon; they are just
> here with only one question
> to ask, which life answers
> by being in them. It is I
> who ask.[4]

---

4 Thomas, R. S., 'Pilgrimages', in *Collected Poems*, p. 364.

My summer visits to Bardsey brought the Island closer so that it began to become a part of me in the same way as my immediate surroundings. Island and mainland are one. As I read more about the history of Bardsey, so it filled out my knowledge of the heritage of the land in which I live. But it was only on my winter visits to the Island that the Sound was finally spanned. A rocky offshore island, secured closely by the sea, is naturally remote and marginal, harsh and liminal. It is a 'desert' place, a fierce landscape, and there are those who travel there for just that reason, as much now as in the past. Here there are few outward distractions for the seeker after God who comes with singleness of purpose. It is a place which can sustain a simple lifestyle albeit demandingly harsh at times, yet it holds within itself a natural microcosm of the whole world. In the winter when the Island is emptied of visitors and only three or four residents remain, it is only then that the hermitage is truly solitary. The 'fast God' is always there before us but, perhaps, there are moments when his absent presence is closer to our arrival than his leaving.

Ten

The Wicklow Hills Beckon

Once again I have been rereading the life of St Seraphim of Sarov. As so often before I pause at the point where Isaiah, the wise old retired abbot, asks Seraphim:

> 'What is it then, this goal of yours?' Isaiah asked. 'I don't know. I keep being pulled back. Now, only sometimes, in the silence, I begin to hear the word that can explain it to me. But I've never listened long enough. I can't, living as I do. So I don't know.'[1]

So Seraphim replies. Yet as I write those words I know this would not be an honest answer if I presumed to make those words mine. There are few things that are being asked of me that prevent me from 'remain in your cell and your cell will teach you all'.

Yet time and again I find myself wandering along paths of the mind, of the imagination, of tasks or meeting with another which I know in my heart are pulling me back, are mitigating the thrust of 'singleness' of purpose. None of these wanderings from the path are bad in themselves. It takes very little for me to find a reason for justifying them, until once again the bubble bursts and I laugh at my own idiocy, at my pomposity and intensity and at how easily I am led astray. Ah, indeed: 'that which I would, I do not' (Rom. 7.15). St John of the Cross succinctly and more lightly described it as 'not gathering flowers on the way', so moving away from

---

1 Beausobre, J. de, 1945, *Flame in the Snow: A Russian Legend*, Constable, p. 104.

St Paul's emphasis on sin. Once again it was a matter of circumventing the route that can so easily spiral down into despondency. I quite deliberately take some 'time out', a deliberate 'gathering of flowers on the way' in order to clear the path yet again. Am I expecting too much of myself in embarking on a way of life, or rather this particular way of life, which is beyond me, even though I sincerely believe it to be under God?

Not many days later after the first serious gale and storm of autumn had blown itself out, I spent much of the morning gardening. As I came back indoors, I switched on the radio to catch the headlines and the room was suddenly filled with a torrent of words and images, pouring out as though from the Tower of Babel. Thinking that I must have mistaken the time and had inadvertently tuned into some lurid radio play, I checked the time which was correct, so I began to pay attention seriously. Minute by minute I listened in disbelief as the commentators appeared to be describing a scene that was unrolling before their very eyes. It was 11 September 2001. The place was New York and in less than half an hour the well-known skyline of Manhattan had disintegrated and the seemingly indestructible twin towers of the World Trade Center – a monument of American stature – had collapsed and their fall was being beamed into all our homes worldwide *as it occurred*. A plane followed closely by another had flown straight into the towers, toppling first one and then the other in a cascade of concrete, glass and human bodies. There had been no warning, no chance to evacuate the building, no way of escape. From one moment to the next in the eyes of the American people and in a knee-jerk reaction, Western civilization as we have known it seemed threatened. This was not war as we had faced so often in the past but an attack by an amorphous 'enemy' we could not identify except in the most general terms of an act of terrorism. Being amorphous it was difficult to engage with directly, a many-headed hydra. That our seemingly sound intelligence services had let us down, that the security systems on which we relied had been infiltrated, became more and more apparent in the following weeks and months.

That afternoon I listened to the heartrending messages that those who had time sent home to their families before the second plane struck the towers or the building collapsed on itself. I listened too, to the accounts of the quasi-'spiritual' training that the terrorists had apparently received as to what should be in their thoughts as they flew into their deaths, deaths that they had chosen and had chosen also for their victims. The language was 'religious' in no uncertain terms, subtle yet strongly doctrinal and brainwashing in the extreme. The contrast yet parity in terms of 'religious' content was chilling, numbing. The dedication of the perpetrators seemed so wholehearted, utterly committed to their cause as they turned murder into what they saw as martyrs' triumph.

Later that night, and during the subsequent days, and not for the first time, my memory took me into uncomfortable areas. What of the Crusades, the Inquisition, the pillage and slaughter of the Reformation and Counter-Reformation? What of the Holocaust? Was not each of these perpetrated in the name of religion and masqueraded as being for the common good? What of present greed and power and genocide, which are not only countenanced in world poverty, famine and ecological exploitation, but have scarcely been acknowledged for what they are? We have barely scratched the surface of facing into some of these even on our very doorsteps as many of us sit comfortably in our affluence. What of the immense unchallenged pressure to conform that this 'society' puts on us? What of my own solitary life, such as it is, and my continual falling short? If I had wondered why I was here, what I was doing with my life in the context of my 'neighbour', I was shot back – forward – into the reality of the present moment, of 'man's inhumanity to man', and 'the point of intersection' as a 'crossing point'. I felt plunged into the depths of this, into an existential depth and darkness into which, at that moment, little light shone. And yet, and yet – there are those last-minute messages sent by the 'victims' of 9/11, those acts of heroism and the sense of community that the immediate aftermath drew out of people who would otherwise never have met, or given one another even a cursory glance. What of them? What of the searching of hearts that stirred so many to prayer and action all over the world?

Since then much has been written about that shattering event. Wiser spirits have perhaps refrained from too many words, allowing the slow process of internalization where the paradox remains unresolved but sharp. Rowan Williams in his brilliant monograph written shortly after having himself been close to the disaster in New York on that day, entitles his thoughts 'writing in the dust' – referring to John 8.6. and Jesus' comment on the woman taken in adultery – as he 'tries to hold that moment for a little longer, long enough for some of our demons to walk away'.[2] For me, as always, it is to 'remain in your cell and your cell will teach you all'.

To remain in my cell in *this place*, in the silence and solitude and space that I had sought and that had been given to me beyond any measure of which I could ever have dreamed. Here there was opportunity, untrammelled by time, to allow 'some of our demons to walk away'. Solitude enables silence to speak to the imagination beyond symbols or signs. In the silence, the immediacy of experience makes space for awe, and in the emptiness of the moment a threshold may be crossed until, once again, it is cloaked by the imagination. Images or words resurface, but there is a silence round them now much as when a student of painting is taught to paint the space *between* or *surrounding* what is seen. For a brief moment I experience this space emptied of the colouring given to it by all that has happened here, the continuity of life: its unique identity. I am emptied of words, which at their best speak from the imagination and hover in awe around this empty space: doors only of entry. But most of the time I sit and watch and wait, living each day in an unknowing and absence which tests me far beyond anything I had ever thought possible. It is grey and full of questions and doubts.

---

2 Williams, Rowan, 2002, *Writing in the Dust: Reflections on 11th September and Its Aftermath*, Hodder & Stoughton, p. 81.

Map 3: Ireland

As I sit gazing out of my window at Bardsey my eyes go to that other offshore island which looks down on me from the poster above my window: Skellig Michael. This northwest peninsula of Wales is rich in holy wells and springs, standing stones and pilgrim churches, but these early artefacts are rare compared to those in some parts of Ireland. My reading had whetted my appetite. An actual visit to the Egyptian or Syrian deserts and a prolonged stay in the desert itself was not an option open to me. (I had seriously considered this in my younger days for, though God is totally present everywhere, some of us have found that exploring certain places and terrains is more conducive to our search than it is for others. Simon Stylites chose the top of a pillar as his 'hermitage', which perhaps freed both the showman in him and his authentic search.) Though the Egyptian desert was no longer a possibility for me maybe a visit to Ireland, a pilgrimage? That was a possibility. I thought long and hard. 'Remain in your cell and your cell will teach you all.' My thoughts would seem to be a direct contradiction of the inmost counsels of my heart. Would this be just a welcome distraction, a very pleasant 'gathering of flowers on the way'? Or was a pilgrimage to Ireland part of the way on which I was being led *in this place*? From time to time most of us need to be stimulated and spiritually nourished by experiences beyond what is given by our immediate surroundings or books. For a solitary, discerning whether it is right to leave her hermitage and the simplicity of her life can be difficult and she may need another to see it more objectively. I had a wise spiritual guide, and finally it seemed right to go and I found the experience enormously enriching and integrating.

The same close friends with whom I had stayed on Bardsey for a week jumped at the idea with characteristic generosity. We planned the route carefully to take in not only pilgrimage sites but also to make it an enjoyable time, for this was also my friends' holiday. Obviously I had no way of knowing where it might be best to stay and the choice seemed endless. There was great hilarity over crossed wires between England and Ireland as the websites, let alone slight differences in language, led to some confusion. We only had ten days, so a pilgrimage on foot had to be transposed into its twenty-first-century counterpart. We flew from Birmingham to Dublin where we took in the Book of Kells as well as the all-pervasive smell of Guinness. Then, hiring a car, we drove south to begin our pilgrimage. The flight seemed to have disorientated me for I commented on how many *Irish* cars seemed to be hogging the road.

Glendalough in the Wicklow hills, which I sometimes see clearly from the headland below Tŷ Pren, was our starting point. Here St Kevin's monastic village lies in its valley between two lakes (from which it takes its name: Glendalough), the equivalent of a Welsh Clas. We entered by the Gateway, the only entrance in the original enclosing circular wall. Spread out before us, over an extensive area and sheltered on three sides by steeply wooded hills and moorland, the monastic village lives on, though now bereft of monks.

It was early in the morning so the 'village' was still empty of other visitors. The site is dominated by St Kevin's Cross and I sat on the grass at its foot close to the still imposing walls and arches of the central monastic church – the 'cathedral' – and allowed the place to speak to me. In the silence it was the *activity* of the life that had been lived here that struck me. Springing from and focused in the daily round of prayer and worship, this was a village self-sufficient in all its needs. It was much larger than the site of the Aberdaron Clas, and almost a village in itself, covering several acres of the fertile valley floor. The monks appeared to have lived singly or in small groups, each stone dwelling or group of dwellings having its own small church. Clustered round the inner community lived the craftsmen, the farm labourers, the masons and the carpenters and their families, an extension of the core community, whatever form that took. The guests were also part of this outer ring, assigned to their own accommodation. (Hospitality is an important part of almost all forms of monastic life, even the strictest.) It is thought that all would have come together for worship at various times, almost certainly for the Sunday celebration of the Eucharist and the vigil that preceded it. I felt as though I was sitting at the hub of a wheel with its many spokes radiating from the centre that both inspired and empowered it. Most surely all the difficulties and cross-currents that affect any diverse group of people living together, however unifying their purpose, would also have been among the 'demons' released here, but was this not also primarily something approaching a gospel-led lifestyle of an authentic simplicity? Here was a simple form of communal life where the skills and gifts of each one furthered the common life of all. In all probability 'they had all things in common' as we read was the lifestyle followed by some of the early converts to Christianity. 'Now the whole group of those who believed were of one heart and soul, and no one claimed private ownership of any possessions, but everything they owned was held in common' (Acts 4.32).

Here, in Glendalough, it was a life lived under the authority of the abbot, who was chosen for his holiness and wisdom, and perhaps, as in the case of St Kevin, for the vision that founded and inspired Glendalough. Here, at its inception, the place of authoritative leadership under God, largely untainted by an underlying drive for power, may have flourished. An abbot, though vested with authority, held that authority in trust. Humility and service go hand in hand with holiness and even as I write these words I realize how counter-cultural they sound. Alas, this early flowering did not last, but fell into corruption and disrepute. But for a time the vision was lived and the 'demons' were recognized and battled with, at least in part. The impact of that early vision lives on among those stones.

Many of the chapels, monks' houses and churches still stand only half ruined, grouped round the 'cathedral' and guarded by a round pencil-tower. These towers, not seen in Wales, may have served both as a place where the monks could take refuge from attack – which explains the only door some many feet from the ground and the windows on every side and level – and also as a bell tower from which the monastery handbell would be rung from a high window for all to hear. Large hanging bells were still un-known. From the top of the tower the whole valley could be seen as well as the surrounding hillsides, so that anyone approaching, whether friend or foe, could not easily remain unseen. There is an extensive burial ground scattered with early, hand-hewn crosses and grave slabs, many tiny ones marking the graves of children, from the simplest stone to a highly intricate High Cross carved with great skill. This garth is still in use, marking a sense of living continuity with this early Celtic Christian community, a link to the present day that we found wherever our pilgrimage led us in Ire-land. Outside the circular enclosing wall lies the nuns' church, or the women's church, in its own enclosure but still an integral part of the whole. And further away still, the small graves of unbap-tized children whose bodies could not be laid to rest in consecrated ground: a sad place.

A little apart there are the remains of St Kevin's cell, known as St Kevin's Bed (a cave), and of a tiny chapel, Templenaskellig (the Church of the Rocks) associated with St Kevin, who later in his life resigned as abbot and moved into solitude. A few of the other monks followed him, also withdrawing to the margins of the communal life to live alone, in eremitical solitude and greater austerity.

I spent many hours sitting or wandering through the ruins, es-pecially early in the mornings. A climb through the trees gave a view over the whole site; the two lakes, the hermitage environs at a distance yet still a part of the whole, artefacts like the Deer stone where the grain was ground, and the small plot of tiny crosses beyond the nuns' church, where the unbaptized children were buried. The whole site was self-contained and self-sufficient yet the life that had been lived here radiated out and does so still. Here, at Glendalough, almost invisible within this secluded valley between the surrounding forested and moorland hills, the monastic tradition of the Desert Fathers flowered on Irish soil and in a remote and fierce landscape.

Walking away from the monastic village along the river, I stumbled on St Saviour's church dating from the twelfth century. Here lies the link between the old order and the new order as in Wales. As the monastic life of Glendalough itself began to fall into decay and disrepute, a group of Augustinian Canons came to the valley under the auspices of the then Bishop of Dublin, and set up a small priory round St Saviour's church at a short distance from the original monastic village. This pattern, moving through the history of medieval Ireland, was repeated over and over again as we journeyed across the island. From the very beginning of our pilgrimage the monastic roots and tradition of the early Celtic Church, its decline and its subsequent 'reform' by the highly organized and centralized western monastic orders, lay mapped out for us.

Leaving Glendalough we made our way from east to west, stopping briefly at Clonmacnoise. This is another monastic village, founded by St Ciarán. Whereas Glendalough was chosen for its natural amenities of water, fertile soil and seclusion, Clonmacnoise was quite literally at the hub of sixth-century Ireland where the east/west artery of communication, the river Shannon, crossed the major north/south land route which ran along the glacial ridge of the hills. This pivotal situation led to the development of Clonmacnoise as a major monastic centre of learning, trade, commerce and political influence. Here was another face of early monasticism where interaction with secular power was evident and the primary thrust of a life of worship, prayer, learning and education became involved with political interests. Clonmacnoise benefited from the patronage of powerful provincial kings but at the price of being drawn into their feuds and aspirations to the kingship of all Ireland. My thoughts switched to the Llŷn Peninsula and St Beuno's monastic Clas at Clynnog Fawr, yet there on Llŷn though the monastery was renowned for the education it provided, it would seem to have kept relatively clear of political involvement for longer despite the patronage under which it flourished.

Our route to County Kerry and my ultimate goal, Skellig Michael, took us via the Burren on the west coast of County Clare. This pause in our pilgrimage, or so we had thought, had been planned deliberately. The Burren is renowned for its amazing flora, which interested all of us. Yet those few days turned out to be pivotal to the pilgrimage itself in ways quite beyond our expectations. The central feature of this remarkable landscape is its fertility and the dramatic contrasts of the terrain over a relatively small area. The name, Burren, is derived from *bhoireann* which means a rocky place. Almost the entire region is based on carboniferous limestone the porous quality of which, when brought into contact with the moulding and melting of the ice-sheets of the last Ice Age, resulted in the bare fissured pavements which are so characteristic of the area. These stretch for miles in certain parts and it would be hard to imagine a more desolate landscape, equivalent in no uncertain terms to a fierce desert terrain. Only once before had I come across similar rocky pavements on a smaller scale, and that was in the Alps at the base of a vast glacier. There they were graphically called 'leichen bretter', or funeral slabs. Scattered over the surface of the flat limestone slabs here on the Burren there are large granite boulders. These much harder rocks rolled about on the surface of the pavements as the ice melted until they became smooth and spherical. They go by the evocative name of *glacial erratics.*

The Burren's coastal climate has extremes of temperature, weather patterns and a high rainfall, all combining to play on the heat-retaining desolate limestone pavements and allowing the fissures to give shelter to an abundance of contrasting flowers such as I had never seen. The area is host to two quite distinct botanical types side by side: the arctic/alpine plants such as gentian and mountain avens, and Mediterranean vegetation such as orchids and maidenhair ferns. Everything was in miniature, each fissure a treasure trove for the botanist and a feast to the eye in the brilliancy of the colours and the intricate detail of the tiny less-known species. We had only to sit on one of the boulders hoping we would not set it in motion, and at our feet there was such an abundance of flowers and ferns that it was hardly necessary for the less agile among us to move on at all.

As we explored the area over the next two days, I realized that this was a landscape which, like Pen Llŷn, held within it a past and a present that spanned hundreds of years of the cultural map of the incoming peoples. Unlike Llŷn, there was a great variety and amazing richness of artefacts that had survived the centuries owing to the hard granite rock, which not only underlay the fertile ground but which had provided the building materials for each successive culture. I felt my roots going back into the past, with which we are all imbued now in the present and which, knowingly or unknowingly, underlies and fashions our thoughts and spiritual bedrock – Jung's 'collective unconscious'. Gradually we became aware that what we were seeing was no 'natural' landscape but one that successive peoples had sculpted carefully to their own ends. Over the centuries the dense forests had been cut down, the clearings grazed and later cultivated, leading eventually to exhaustion and erosion of the land and the many bare hilltops and limestone pavements as the people moved on. But everywhere artefacts remain of each successive culture.

The primary purpose of this pilgrimage for me was to delve more deeply into the Celtic Christian past of our islands, but here was laid out also the pre-Christian past. This past was part of the rich heritage into which Christianity came and from which it took many aspects, baptizing them into a Christian framework. Does not every people live and reflect the essence of our shared human condition, and do not all religions give meaning to the longing and desires of humanity according to the cultures of the age?

Here in this part of western Ireland there appear to be no traces of the earliest peoples, who had arrived from Britain and from mainland Europe probably 6,000 years ago in the Mesolithic period. By 3000 BC, in the Neolithic period, there begins to be plenty of evidence of human settlements. The portal dolmens still stand, bare now of the earth which used to cover them and the dead who lay buried there. They are enormous; a man standing under them is dwarfed to insignificance. How were these huge stones moved and erected let alone lifted?

The transition from the Stone Age to the Bronze Age is marked by a change in how the people buried their dead. Wedge-shaped gallery graves that resemble a huge box, using boulders every bit as vast as the earlier dolmens became the norm. A man standing inside one of these is as dwarfed as by the earlier portal dolmen. Middens and cooking areas can be found round these sites throwing up evidence of what these people ate and how they cooked. Fossilized skulls and bones and even grains, primitive stone implements, smoke-charred cooking stones – all are clues for the archaeologists of the period. Later still came the hundreds of stone enclosures, or ring forts, which span many centuries and vary from hill-forts to cliff-top forts guarding small family units or much larger settlements, some with quite sophisticated layout and fortifications. Again I was reminded of the fine Iron Age fort of Tre'r Ceiri on the Rivals on the north coast of Llŷn near Caernarfon, where it is possible to sense an antiquity and power that resonates with the depths of our past.

With the arrival of the Celts in Ireland about 600 BC, there is evidence of a sudden explosion in the number of settlements in the Burren. Celtic culture has been described as the 'the fine flower of the Iron Age'. Celtic society was highly stratified. Each tribal territory had its own chieftain, who might also owe allegiance to a high king. Under the chieftain came the warriors, the aristocracy of the tribe, below whom were the priests and the poets and historians (the precursors in Wales of the Welsh Bardic tradition), and the artists. Then came the bottom rung of the freemen or small farmers. Women and children were rarely mentioned, if at all. Below all of these came the serfs, parallel in standing to the serfs and slaves of medieval Europe. The Celts appeared to have been a very vigorous and active peoples and much given to storytelling, feasting and drinking. This gave rise to an oral tradition carrying a richness of culture that grew out of the very soil they inhabited. Theirs was no following in the footprints of earlier peoples but an *inhabiting* that linked them to the land in a unity which our contemporary society in the West has all but lost. This sense of unity is of great importance to me also and is a pivotal element of my life here in Pen Llŷn: this sense of a oneness with the land, the *place*, an 'inhabiting'. For so many nowadays, the place where we live would not bear the weight of being the place we *inhabit*. Even the house in which we live may feel far from being where we feel 'at home'. Our society is marked by a mobility that has taken us away from our familial roots through the need to find work or a house that is within our means – or perhaps a breakdown of relationships has dictated a move. Even health can be a factor. The sense of 'inhabiting' a place in the way former generations often did, is rare for us now. The younger generation often migrate to new continents.

It is now clear that Christianity had reached Ireland certainly by the early years of the fifth century, that is, before St Patrick. By the fifth century Christianity had spread sufficiently over large areas of Ireland from the Continent and Britain for Pope Celestine I to send Palladius from Gaul as bishop in 431, only two years after he had sent Germanus to Wales, both in the context of combating Pelagianism.

We found many ruined early medieval churches which had obviously been built on the sites of much earlier places of worship. They were of a simple design that was almost barn-like, with strong rectangular walls supporting a stone roof and a purely functional square doorway in the west wall. In one place there were some unusual triangular tent-shaped shrines, which, it is thought, may have held the remains of a local saint or holy man. There were also many examples of settlements clustered round these early churches, which were in large part monastic.

We took a boat over to the Aran Islands, off the coast of Co. Clare, where the people still retain something of the crofting life of earlier years. Here, also, we found the remains of many Celtic Christian churches, parts of sculpted High Crosses and grave slabs; interestingly also, the graves of three Roman soldiers identified by the 'sword cross' used on the slab that marked their resting place. It is thought that the Romans never penetrated so far west in Ireland, but possibly these three were shipwrecked off the coast and as Christians were given a Christian burial.

Ireland and its people are enigmatic in ways that even our short visit so far had thrown into sharp relief. I had visited several times, 30-odd years before, but during the past 20 years in solitude my perceptions had begun to alter, and Ireland itself had certainly altered in those years. There was now a relative affluence made possible by large grants from the European Union. Modern bungalows had replaced many of the crofts so typical of former years, bungalows with no specifically Irish feel to them. In Dublin, and no doubt in other urban centres, interesting modern buildings had grown up cheek by jowl with the beautiful Georgian crescents by the river Liffey. Most of the old tenements and appalling slums had been cleared. But the people remained the same: friendly, welcoming and humorous. I warmed to this land and its people. But the best was still to come.

I will arise and go now, and go to Innisfree,
And a small cabin build there, of clay and wattles made:
Nine-bean rows will I have there, a hive for the honey-bee,
And live alone in the bee-loud glade.

And I shall have some peace there, for peace comes dropping slow,
Dropping from the veils of the morning to when the cricket sings;

There midnight's all a glimmer, and noon a purple glow,
And evening full of the linnet's wings.

I will arise and go now, for always night and day
I hear lake water lapping with low sounds by the shore;
While I stand on the roadway, or on the pavements grey,
I hear it in the deep heart's core.[3]

3 Yeats, W. B., 1890, 'The Lake Isle of Innisfree', published in the *Irish National Observer*.

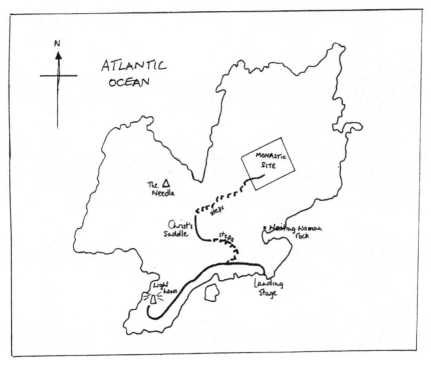

Map 4: Ireland and Skellig Michael (St. Michael's Rock)

Eleven

That Other Island –
Skellig Michael

We only had three days left of our pilgrimage as we set out from
Co. Clare down the west coast to Co. Kerry for what had been
for me the ultimate goal of our pilgrimage: Skellig Michael. The
weather had been amazingly good through all the past week. Not a
drop of rain had we seen, which for Ireland, particularly along its
western coast, is well nigh unheard of. Now the forecast sounded
more unsettled. Would we arrive at Ballinskelligs – our chosen
jumping-off point for Skellig Michael rather than the more popular Valentia Island – and reach our goal, or would we arrive only
to be within reach and perhaps just see the Skelligs on the horizon
with a turbulent Atlantic guarding the island and denying access?
This was the scene that greets so many who travel the pilgrim route
of Llŷn only to find that at the end of their pilgrimage they have
to be content with a view of Bardsey from the slopes of Mynydd
Mawr at the tip of the Peninsula, the crossing denied them by the
stormy waters of the Sound.

The drive down the west coast and across the mouth of the
Shannon by ferry was beautiful. All was bathed in sunshine. We
decided to play the tourist and make first for Valentia Island,
which we reached in good time. Portmagee would have been an alternative place from which to take a boat to Skellig Michael but we
had opted for the tiny, less well-known fishing village of Ballinskelligs, set a little further south along the coast on the Ring of Kerry.
Boats left from there also, but they were simpler without all the

luxury and tourist additions offered by the service from Valentia
Island. We had decided to break our journey here in order to visit
the Skellig Experience Visitor Centre. This modern interpretation-
centre with its 80-seat theatre transports the visitor to the island
by means of models, graphics and artefacts, and a filmed audio-
visual presentation. I found it engrossing, showing in detail what
had been pieced together through meticulous research of the life
and times of those early Christian monks in the island monasteries
of the west coast of Ireland. The centre's 15-minute audio-visual
programme is a guided tour of ancient and contemporary Skellig Michael complete with a crew of incongruous white-habited
monks in a high-prowed boat, rowing valiantly out to the island
to the accompaniment of haunting Irish harp music and singing;
all a glorious jumble of Irish history and folklore. Nonetheless it
was a foretaste of what awaited us. The filming was so graphic in
its depiction of a stormy 13km crossing and the subsequent steep
ascent from the landing place to the plateau just below the summit
182m above, that one of our number decided there and then that
this was not for him. Anyone who suffers from sea-sickness and/or
vertigo is strongly advised against setting out.

My reading combined with the excellent presentations in the
Centre painted a unique picture of this offshore island and the
monks that had sought it out as 'their place of resurrection', that
same evocative phrase that echoes through all the annals of early
Celtic monasticism in these islands. Here, on this twin-peaked
crag 217m high, battered and embattled by the sea and at that
time a day's journey from the mainland, lay a wild and fierce place
where prayer and worship could be offered in total solitude and
the demons could be fought. Access was as formidable as was the
challenge of building shelter from the winds and storms. The first
monks cut steps in the rock from three alternative inlets all the
way up to the plateau 182m above. The alternative landing places
were essential because of the weather, the storms and the direction of the wind which could veer from one compass point to another with little warning. On the plateau itself the monks built six

beehive huts, two oratories and a circular graveyard. Two cisterns collected rainwater from the mountain slope above the site – there are no natural springs – and these cisterns were connected to the huts by culverts, a water system that is still in working order today.

A small area immediately below the huts appears to have been cleared of stones to form a meagre kitchen garden. There is only a shallow layer of soil on the island, barely sufficient to sustain the turf that probably supplied at least a little fuel for fires and extra roof protection for the huts. Corn could only have come from the mainland during the short summer months when a window in the weather allowed boats to make the hazardous crossing and land in one of the coves slightly sheltered from the lashing waves that guarded the solitude of the island. The monks' diet was restricted to what this bare rock offered: fish and possibly seal meat with the blubber supplying oil, shellfish and sea birds and their eggs, supplemented by the little the monks were able to grow themselves. We can only hazard a guess at how many lost their lives to the sea as they fished or scrambled up and down the rocks to pillage the birds' nests – the graveyard has not been excavated. The huts themselves have needed very little restoration, having been so well and sturdily constructed. The beehive structure resists all pressures as any force of wind or rain only serves to pack the stones more tightly. The construction of this monastic site itself is almost unbelievable, but the cutting of the steps in the rock face from inlets to the plateau stretches incredulity still further. Only one of these step-ways is still negotiable: 600 stone steps with, in places, a sheer drop on both sides to the churning sea below. This is not a place where any but the most robust and single-minded could have survived.

It is difficult to put an exact date on the founding of this semi-communal island monastery but the buildings are similar to others on Ireland's west coast, some of which are better documented. The early sixth century is the date agreed by most. By AD 795, it is known that the Vikings from Scandinavia first launched their attacks on the Irish coast. The *Annals of Innisfallen, of Ulster, and of the Four Masters* all record attacks on Skellig Michael. In 812 the monastery was sacked and in 823 there was a further attack when Etgal, Abbot of Skellig, was taken and starved to death. Yet the monks always returned.

Not content with the rigours offered by the life of the Skellig monastery, one monk moved himself to a hermitage on the southern peak that could only be reached through a dangerously narrow needle's eye in the rock. According to the highly imaginative and fictional account in Geoffrey Moorhouse's book, *Sun Dancing*, this monk lost his reason and died a grisly death. Those who have risked life and limb more recently and climbed the pinnacle beyond the needle's eye, witness to the possible traces of a hermit's cave. There are further entries in the *Annals* of this period which continue until the mid-eleventh century. These include one recording the baptism of Olav of Norway, later to become King Olav II, which throws light on the importance and veneration for holiness in which these remote island monasteries were held. In the twelfth century, the ever-reliable and much-travelled historian Gerald of Wales writes that the monks of Skellig Michael had moved to the mainland Augustinian monastery of Ballinskellig, witnessing to the same reform and revitalizing of the monastic tradition through the western established orders that is recorded throughout the fringe of these western regions.

Later in medieval times another chapel was added to the monastic site on Skellig Michael, sure evidence that visits to the island continued after the resident monks had left. These visits were probably made by pilgrims and possibly also by monks from the mainland who may have spent Lent there. Later accounts in the annals are scant and often scurrilous, as the annual pilgrimages in Holy Week became an ideal opportunity for courting couples. Finally, in the nineteenth century these pilgrimages were denounced and ceased. This stood in sharp contrast to Gerald of Wales' description recorded in medieval terms:

In the south of Munster near Cork there is a certain island of Saint Michael, revered for its true holiness from ancient times.

There is a certain stone there outside of, but almost touching the door of the church on the right-hand side. In a hollow on the upper part of this stone, there is found every morning through the merits of the saints of this place, as much wine as is necessary for the celebration of as many Masses as there are priests to say Mass on that day there.

Leaving Valentia Island we arrived in Ballinskelligs in brilliant sunshine and were rewarded by a walk out to Bolus Head with a fine view of the Skelligs. The two islands rose steeply from the sea, rocky pyramids on the distant horizon, beckoning and luring us, siren-like, to step out onto the deep to the edge of the world. That evening I read more about the island.

A shipwreck of about 1400 BC is the first known mention of Skellig when, in the legends of Miletius a leader of early invasions of Ireland, he is recorded as having lost two sons in the area.

> Irr lost his life upon the western main;
> Skellig's high cliffs the hero's bones contain.
> In the same wreck Arranan too was lost,
> Nor did his corpse e'er touch Ierne's coast.

Other early stories tell of those who fled to Skellig for refuge from pursuing enemies from as far afield as Bangor in N. Ireland, from where St Malachy is said to have fled his monastery in the fifth century.

The earliest Christian records of Skellig Michael place it securely within the Celtic monastic tradition. Over and over again we see that the western seaboard of Ireland, Scotland and Wales were the desert/wildernesses of these lands in terms of the monastic desert tradition that had been planted there certainly by the fifth century. Here in Ireland it was a centrifugal movement as it had been for those early Desert Fathers: a fleeing from the towns and cities, a fleeing from the 'world' and all its perceived evils. By their flight their lives spoke of being *in the world*, part of the world, but not *of the world.* Theirs was a contemplative life in the extreme. This was in sharp contrast to some of the later monastic foundations such as Clonmacnoise, which gradually evolved into a monastic city much involved with the political and commercial movements of the times, or even Glendalough, which was a hive of activity. These early monks and hermits in the desert tradition searched for God not only on the margins of society but at the extremities of the known world. They saw this not as a negation of a shared humanity but as a positive search. It was not a rejection but a deliberate return to the land. In the fierce landscape of the western seaboard with its rocky and rugged terrain at the very brink of the earth, they had no need to devise an ascetic life. On Skellig Michael there was no other life possible, separated as they were from the mainland. The western horizon was all they saw as the sun set and each day died at what was to them, the edge of the world. They could flee no further.

From Bolus Head, we were also looking into the setting sun and there was Skellig Michael lying out on the horizon, 13km from the mainland. There it was: a rocky peak in a vast and turbulent sea, invincible, its summit lost in the sky, the highest point closest to the heavens above. And beyond lay an empty horizon: 3,000 miles of Atlantic, as we now know. For those first monks this spare and rugged rock could have been none other than the extreme desert place that they sought, where they did battle with the 'demons' of this world, the demons that they found within themselves. Perhaps from the very beginning it became known as St Michael's rock: Michael, the Archangel of spiritual conflict. It was Michael, the Archangel of the Book of Revelation who waged war in heaven against Satan and defeated him, throwing him down to the earth. Ever since, this enemy has tried to plant and foster deception deep in the heart of each and all of us – an allegorical account that fits human experience only too well. It is because of this that Michael has come to epitomize the 'war' that we wage as our demons are transformed. There are two other island-monasteries dedicated to St Michael on the western coastal fringe: St Michael's Mount,

Cornwall and the other St Michael off the coast of Brittany. Here, as there, was the same three-tiered universe and seemingly dualistic early medieval spirituality with which I was already so familiar. I was transported back over hundreds of years to the sixth century and those first monks and then further back still, for the rock on which we were standing, the headland all around us as on the island itself, is 350 million years old. The sunset highlighted the red of this granite hard sandstone and the blues and greens of the embedded slate. Centuries against the background of millions of years become a gateway of eternity.

Next morning I woke early. A veiled light shone weakly through the curtains. Outside the world had vanished, cloaked by a white mist. Waiting for breakfast no one spoke. The landlady bustled in brightly with coffee, eggs and bacon, toast and marmalade and, reading our silence, met it with a smile. 'It will be a perfect day, the sea choppy perhaps, but that will just add spice to your crossing to the islands.' An hour later we were down at the jetty watching the boat being readied for putting out to sea and eyeing with some alarm one of the two young men to whom we were about to entrust our lives, who was quite obviously hung-over from some revels of the previous night. However the other – Declan – seemed bright enough. It was a well-appointed boat with all the necessary equipment for depth-sounding and radar, radio contact, lifejackets and an inflatable dinghy so that the landlubber among us, who was going to make the most of his solitary day exploring the immediate area, felt reassured and waved us off with seeming calm detachment. A solitary heron fishing off a nearby rock hardly deigned to raise its head to follow the sound of our sputtering engine and slow getting under way as we left the jetty behind.

As we rounded Bolus Head and pointed out to the open sea, the boat began to buck, rising and falling in a slithering slide with each surmounted wave. It was certainly choppy. Unlike the crossing of the Bardsey Sound, this crossing was over the open Atlantic and also four times longer, heightening our anticipation. The three peaks of Great Skellig – Skellig Michael, Little Skellig and Lemon

Rock – rose far off on the horizon, beckoning, and luring us away from the mainland. As the land receded so the swell increased. Up we rose, riding smoothly, almost gently, to poise for a moment before pitching down the other side.

The remnants of the morning's mist began to lift and sky and sea burst into life. We were soon being followed by a school of dolphins that dived and surfaced, seemingly oblivious of the swell but making the most of the shoal of fish that the boat had attracted. The sky held the early morning colours of the rising sun. The birds circled above us, needing to break their night's fast and to carry food home to their nest-sitting mates and hungry hatchlings. The land-hugging cormorants were soon left behind. Among the great black-backed, heron and common gulls, the neater fulmars and kittiwakes swooped and dived. Further out still Manx shearwaters, razorbills, guillemots and gannets flew by, some as though they were intent on reaching a destination from which nothing would deflect them. Others flew more haphazardly, circling or climbing high above us before plummeting into the sea to resurface some distance away with a fish in their beaks or empty-beaked. For me this was like home from home, but on a grander scale. The light began to strengthen and suddenly the sun broke through transforming sea and sky into a shimmering blue expanse only broken here and there by a cloud that laid its shadow on the water. At the same time I became aware of a new bird: small and stumpy with short wings that beat so fast it gave the impression of a clockwork toy whirring over the water. As these flew closer and closer to the boat my heart skipped a beat: dozens of puffins whirred around us, their multicoloured beaks startlingly bright in the sparkling light.

The islands drew nearer and seals replaced the dolphins, peering up at us from their wise old-man faces and round inquisitive eyes. Once I thought I saw a basking shark, its triangular fin cutting through the waves, but that could have been imagination much heightened by the charged atmosphere I felt growing around me. Those first monks putting out to sea in maybe only fragile skin covered coracles and short paddles, how had they survived this crossing? Or did they use sturdier craft with high prows and stronger hulls, as we had seen in the film on Valentia Island? Were their hearts singing or sinking within them in rhythm with the oars and waves? Did the vision of the island as their goal and the place where they hoped to pray and fast, defeat the demons and send Satan tumbling down into the sea overcoming their natural fear and spurring them on? Their stories and hagiographies, written many years later, paint an idealized picture of the spiritual hero as interpreted at that time. Yet in a very real sense they probably could not have turned back even if their nerve had failed them, for they were at the mercy of the seas in their frail craft. Out there, halfway between the mainland and Skellig Michael, a kaleidoscope of images flashed past my inner eye, gradually resolving into the singleness of purpose that I could only dimly echo, which lay in the hearts of those first pilgrim-monks. Romanticism would have had no place then as it had no place now, only a reaching beyond the known, beyond any definable hope, or any concepts or words of interpretation, into a dimension that transcends time. Though those first monks who had set out for Skellig were almost certainly aiming for the island as their destination, there was also another tradition prevalent at that time. A small group of monks or even just one on his own would set out from the coast of the mainland with *no* fixed destination. Wherever their craft took them, the first landfall that they reached was, for them, the place to which God had led them, and it was there that they would find their 'place of resurrection'.

We had passed Lemon Rock and were now drawing level with Little Skellig. The noise and the stench that reached us all at once from the island were overpowering. From the mainland Little Skellig had looked benign enough, the only strange thing about it being what appeared to be the unusual striated rock of its cliff. As we drew nearer this came into sharp focus. Every ledge was crowded by thousands of nesting gannets, while in the air above them thousands more circled waiting to take their turn at incubating the single egg that each pair lays. Their chalky guano splashing the rocks below them accounted for the seemingly striated appearance of the rock. The smell was overpowering. Gannet's eggs are so shaped that they do not roll off the narrow ledges that serve as 'nests'. Each pair lays only one egg and both parents share the long period of incubation. They do this by, first one parent and then the other, balancing the egg between their webbed feet so that it nestles under the warm down of their breasts. At changeover time an intricate dance of faultless choreography transfers the egg from parent to parent, something we were hoping to see on our return journey when we would draw closer to Little Skellig.

The sea was calmer now. All that I had seen and absorbed on the crossing formed a rich backdrop for what was still to come. Had the wind got up we knew we would not be able to land but only at best circle the island before returning to the mainland while it was still safe to do so. But we approached the landing stage in almost ideal conditions and wobbling on our sea legs disembarked thankfully to feel dry land under our feet once more.

It was not until after we had left the concrete road which led from the landing stage to the lighthouse that the ascent began up the monks' steps. The large notice at the beginning of the steps issued a dire warning to anyone with heart trouble, breathing problems or who suffered from vertigo, *not* to attempt the climb. Sobered but undeterred we began to climb, singly and in silence, each at their own pace. The air around us was anything but silent at first until we had climbed beyond the screaming of the gulls at sea level, and the throbbing of the boat's engine had ceased to drum in our heads. I hung back until I was able to climb alone. This was holy ground.

I climbed steadily and lightly. The solitude and the silence were in no way solemn; no brow-furrowing concentration was needed, not at all. The island seemed to take us to itself so that I felt immediately that I was a part of all that surrounded me. It was almost intoxicating. I gazed with incredulity at the paved steps as they stretched up and up above me, and at the puffins that waddled in and out of their burrows at my very feet. They eyed me without a trace of fear, almost oblivious of my presence, in fact so oblivious that as they came in to land they relieved themselves in no uncertain terms, taking no account of where their white squit would land. It is many years since the wildlife on the island had fallen prey to men who hunted it down for food so we humans had become just another living presence sharing the same living space. I climbed on and became conscious of the rocks falling away from either side of the steps. Daring to stop on a wider firmer step, I gazed down at the sea now many metres below me, the water dashing against the rocks throwing spray high into the air. On a promontory to my right stood a solitary rock known as the Wailing Woman, hinting perhaps at legends from the not so distant past, for even now, and from a distance, there is a sense of sorrow and death that hangs in the air around that rock. Here, it is often told, an unwary tourist had stepped back to take yet another even more impressive photo and . . .

I climbed more slowly now as the gradient increased. The puffins had long since been left behind, the vegetation was sparse: a ground cover of a fleshy-leaved trailing plant with tiny pink flowers which I had never seen before. Here and there a clump of coarse grass clung to a crevice in the rocks but soon even these ceased and the steps now were hewn out of the rock face itself. There was a short respite as I reached Christ's Saddle, a small flat green area, where we could draw breath and look around in comparative comfort with no sheer drop on any side. From here there is a view of the Needle – the south pinnacle of the island – and the Needle's Eye through which had lain the hermitage. I resumed the climb once more. The lines of the rocks were all in verticals now, rugged, broken, unyielding. The steps joined the vertical ascent until they took a turn to the right. A light mist had rolled in from the sea and the sense of space and distance was lost. I followed the path to the right and found myself at the foot of what looked like a retaining wall and a narrow tunnel. As I entered the darkness of the tunnel, the sun broke through once more sending my shadow before me as I stepped out into the monastic enclosure.

The beehive huts and oratories lay before me as they have stood through all the centuries. Silhouetted against the sky were the Priest's Cross and the smaller rough-hewn crosses of the monks' graveyard. Little Skellig lay beyond, out to sea and beyond that the faint outline of the mainland coast.

> This is where the guide books stop and the poems
> begin. This is where we have to imagine the monks
> seeing only the sky with nothing
> between themselves and heaven, and their Psalter
> for food, the rain for drink, and possibly
> a strip of wheat beyond the enclosure. This desert
> is on the edge of the ocean, and in a precarious
> world, they made the edge a virtue.[1]

No one spoke. The way out was hidden behind a protecting rock. We were alone, each one wrapped in his or her own thoughts.

There was a guide who respected those first minutes of silence. Then he recounted the historical and archaeological facts with no attempt at poetic or romantic interpretation, keeping himself in the background, letting the place speak for itself. The stones tell their own story. He gave us dates and figures: the enclosure measured a mere 30 x 100 metres with a sheer drop of 182 metres down to the sea. The largest of the corbelled beehive huts was surprisingly spacious: 4.5 x 4 metres and 5 metres high, the walls over 1 metre thick – considerably larger than my own small cabin. Stone pegs protrude halfway up the wall indicating the possibility that there may once have been an upper floor. There were two small window openings to the east and west which would have given light to this upper storey, while at ground level the only opening was the low and narrow door. Were these early monks smaller

---

1 Scott, David, 2002, 'Skellig Michael', in *Sabbatical Poems*, published privately, p. 22. (The final version of this poem can be found in Scott, David, 2005, *Piecing Together*, Bloodaxe Books.)

than we are now or was the lowness of the opening mainly to keep out the elements? There were two recesses for storage space and traces of smoke in the doorway possibly indicating some attempt at smoking fish for winter use. The other huts were a little smaller. The larger of the two oratories is boat shaped and has a window facing east and traces of a stone altar. It is built to give onto the graveyard which clusters round the Priest's Cross and the smaller rough-hewn crosses. The smaller oratory lies at a little distance from the main group of buildings on an artificially constructed platform only protected from the sheer drop at the cliff's edge by a low retaining wall. One would certainly have had to be sure-footed and confident to live here. The medieval church is all but ruined apart from its eastern window aperture. The only other building is a small square structure, neatly roofed, which stands in the 'outer garden' and was apparently, a medieval lavatory. I wish I had investigated this! Three small terraced areas show traces of cultivation on a frugal scale. Just above the monastery there are indications of a cooking area and also a possible pre-Christian site.

I detached myself from the group – we were about a dozen peo-ple – and wandered into the main cell and sat alone in the semi-darkness. I might have been in a cave in the bowels of the earth, all my senses whittled down, and yet there was still that unseen sense of there being nothing but the vault of the sky above me and the sheer drop of the pinnacle of rock falling away to the sea all round me. I knelt in the oratory and as my eyes adapted to the light, gazed out over the sea through the small east window and had the same sense of the solid rock on which I knelt, and yet of being poised between the sky and the bowels of the earth. In the graveyard I was not alone, though who they were, the angel-spirits that surrounded me, I do not know. I sensed them in the same way as I had become conscious of the angels of Llŷn round Tŷ Pren. I climbed above the monastery where the earth held the presence of even older footprints. Below me the site had begun to empty and for a few brief minutes I was alone. Nothing stirred. There was no sound, no movement in the emptiness. In the stillness it was as though, 'I heard a voice I had not heard before' (Ps. 81.6).

We had our picnic on Christ's saddle in glorious sunshine, hardly speaking, filled by the day's experiences that would take many years to integrate.

Let Bernard Shaw have the last word: 'Skellig Michael, 10 miles off the Kerry coast . . . Whoever has not stood in the graveyard on the summit of that cliff among the beehive dwellings and their beehive oratory does not know Ireland through and through.'

Shaw was so bowled over by his visit to Skellig Michael that he writes again in a letter to a friend:

> . . . there are 90 fathoms under the sea out of which the Great Skellig rushes up 700 feet so suddenly that you have to go straight up stairs to the top – over 600 steps. And at the top amazing beehives of flat rubble stones, each overlapping the one below until the circle meets in a dome – cells, oratories, churches, and outside them cemeteries, wells, crosses, all clustering like shells on a prodigious rock pinnacle, with precipices sheer down on every hand, and lodged on the projecting stones overhanging the deep huge stone coffins made apparently by giants, and dropped there God knows how. . . . I tell you the thing does not belong to any world that you or I have lived or worked in: it is part of a dream world. . . . I hardly feel real again yet.

Twelve

Transplanting

'You must give birth to your images. They are the future waiting to be born . . . The future must enter into you long before it happens. Just wait for the hour, the birth of new clarity.' (*Rainer Maria Rilke*)

As the summers pass into autumn and winter there seem to be fewer intervals between the storms as they sweep in from the Atlantic. The wind, too, rarely holds its breath, seeming never to blow itself out, always storing up something for the next day. Is this part of global warming or is it also coloured by the changing rhythms of my own life as I move well beyond the biblical three score years and ten? Certainly the fierceness of the elements and the challenges of the sheer physical demands of this *place* seem to increase. Now that I am less able physically and joints certainly make themselves felt, I need to see where I can simplify my life still further. Ageing is an unknown process until it arrives for each of us.

After 25 years a move becomes not only inevitable but comes towards me not so much as a threat with the finality of an ending as an invitation – a continuation of the journey in another place as yet unknown. In fantasy I had hoped I might die here and add my twenty-first-century bones to those in whose footsteps I had trodden – a purely romantic daydream. I remembered how Sr Helen Mary, the hermit on Bardsey, had hoped for just the same. In reality the journeys that make up this narrative are drawing towards a conclusion as the nub of these interweaving stories is *this place* centred on Pen Llŷn around Tŷ Pren and its close environs. Yet on another level my personal solitary journey will continue wherever my life takes me, whether I continue living quite alone or more among other people. So I felt at peace. Or so it was at first. While there is no definite place to which to move the inevitable remains a concept without substance and the imagination is happy to live in the present hooked into a delusion of freedom from angst.

For the past year I have felt my roots in this cabin and the surroundings loosening, that is in this *immediate place*, yet at the same time their anchorage in my own being strengthening. When I try to put flesh onto the bones of a move my hope is to find somewhere in the area where I can continue to explore the solitary life *here* but in gentler surroundings, with a few of the more essential amenities nearer at hand. There might even be somewhere with a little more shelter from the worst of the fierceness of the elements, though anywhere on the coastal fringes of Pen Llŷn does wind well. The elements and the natural world have been so intimately bound up with my journey, but slightly less of a challenge on that level would not now come amiss.

For some years now when I have been asked how I live, how do I pray? Do I have a rule; a timetable; how do I spend my time? I have come to reply: 'I just live here.'[1] There is nothing special or spiritualized about a solitary life. It is just one way of responding in faith to God. Every life has a rhythm punctuated by the need to eat and to sleep, to work and to relax with enjoyment or sadness, contentment or anxiety. It is no different for a hermit.

Once again I needed to look at the essentials of my eremitic life, and once again this proved to be a salutary experience in honesty. Silence and solitude are a means to an end not an end in themselves; to be safeguarded, yes, but not idolized nor idealized. Where we live is also important, more so for some than for others. But often

---

1 I owe this reply to one given by an unknown monk on Mt Athos and retold by Brother Colin CSWG.

there is no choice and if, as we age, we have not internalized much of our life's journey, then the thought of an uprooting – a move – will feel like the end of the road and the future could look very threatening. I have laboured the theme of the connection between a fierce landscape and the eremitic life until the reader's patience must have been sorely tried. But now with the approach of old age does this still figure or has its work been done? Gradually the outer storms or calm and the inner struggles, *penthos*[2] or peace, become more integrated and are no longer concepts but a part of 'just living'. The artificial barrier between outer and inner begins to dissolve in an ordinary everyday sense, bringing a deeper awareness of unity. Life simplifies. The invisible One seems to become even more invisible but the darkness and seeming nothingness may yield an occasional sense of what St John of the Cross encapsulated in *Toda – Nada*: *Toda* meaning everything, the gift, and *Nada* nothing, the empty space.

What is prayer? What is life? What is work as 'opposed to prayer'? Yet 'life is prayer and prayer is life'. These dichotomies have become so ingrained in our Western psyches. The fragility of our identities can be much accentuated within the complexity of our contemporary culture. It was Alasdair MacIntyre who wrote:

> modernity partitions each human life into a variety of segments, each with its own norms and modes of behaviour. So work is divided from leisure, private life from public, the corporate from the personal. So both childhood and old age have been wrenched away from the rest of human life and made over into distinct realms. And all these separations have been achieved so that it is the distinctiveness of each and not the unity of the life of the individual who passes through those parts in terms of which we are taught to think and feel.[3]

---

2 Penthos: awareness of sin with contrition.
3 MacIntyre, Alasdair, 1985, *After Virtue: A Study in Moral Theory*, 2nd corrected edn, Duckworth, p. 204.

Yet inevitably my thoughts do return to my move and I see the essentials of my own life distilled now as somewhere where I can live simply with as great a measure of solitude and silence as may be possible. It will be a bonus if there is some access to the beauty of natural surroundings whether it be a garden, a view or even a few pot plants, if wide open spaces are no longer within easy reach. Living on the edge of a village community would bring a different sense of local belonging but hopefully this would fall into place given time and without fuss. This as yet immaterial new anchorage will be 'where I live' and key words are: flexibility and a ready sense of humour. Simplicity is incompatible with taking oneself too seriously and so occupying centre stage, an ever-present danger for a hermit or anyone living alone. A wise old monk – Sebastian Moore OSB – wrote recently that the continual inner chatter with ourselves is really nonsensical. There is only one 'me' and not the two who seem to be in continual dialogue.

As I write I am looking out onto headland and Sound and the concepts begin to dissolve as words block the freedom of flow. Gradually my life, which has been so closely bound up with my surroundings and the flow of the past, returns to the present moment and rejoins the flow.

A year passed and nothing possible came up that was not as inaccessible as Tŷ Pren. Was I misinterpreting the signs? Was I to move away to quite new surroundings? Was I in fact continuing to hold on to the controls? My unreal sense of peace was broken open and I gazed into a future which loomed uncertainly, rather like the deepening shadow that had come towards me as a vast wall from the southwesterly horizon at the eclipse of the sun. Here was a challenge that was so open-ended that my roots were shaken further and I was thoroughly buffeted by each day's prevailing wind. Of course these are the hurdles that almost all of us meet at some time in our lives so why all this fuss? But a move is always disturbing especially after 25 years; my inner voice comes up with a ready excuse. In the Sound the tide-race made eddies and whirlpools round the offshore rocks; in my heart conflicting feelings dashed me against the hard rocks of reality where they splintered and found the deeper clefts of my vulnerability. The less than confident person who had embarked on this solitary quest over a quarter of a century ago was as evident as ever.

Summer was drawing towards autumn once again and I found myself dreading the thought of approaching winter. Several people offered help with lifts and shopping, realizing that carrying provisions across the fields from town to bus and bus to Tŷ Pren was becoming increasingly difficult. But once I become reliant on others I feel I could soon be a burden and this sits uneasily, however willing the offers of help. This is not a day and age of faith when a hermit is automatically supported by the local community. To move became more urgent before the time came 'when to go up hill is an ordeal and a walk is something to dread' (Eccles. 12.5 JB).

Trust had fled. My 'outer cell' – Tŷ Pren – began to feel more like a prison than the place of blessing it had become over the years, however difficult the journey had been at times. I was no longer at home to myself and therefore also not to God. I was scattered.

An old man was living in a (disused) temple and the demons came to say to him, 'Leave this place which belongs to us,' and the old man said, 'No place belongs to you.' Then they began to scatter his palm leaves about one by one, and the old man went on gathering them together with perseverance. A little later the devil took his hand and pulled him to the door but he seized the lintel with the other hand crying out, 'Jesus, save me.' Immediately the devil fled away. Then the old man began to weep. Then the Lord said to him, 'Why are you weeping?' And the old man said, 'Because the devils have dared to seize a man and treat him like this.' The Lord said to him, 'You had been careless. As soon as you turned to me again, you see I was beside you.'[4]

---

4 Ward, Benedicta SLG, 1975, *The Sayings of the Desert Fathers*, Mowbray, p. 61.

At last I began to let go and trust more fully once again. Our masks do not fool God though we may allow them to fool ourselves or to project our own splintered selves onto others. Gradually and tentatively I began to return to myself and a renewed sense of hope found houseroom once more.

The way began to open up. A small cottage was offered me for the community to rent. It lies on the edge of Aberdaron, at the end of a quiet cul de sac yet only two minutes from the centre of the village and beach, church, shop and bus. Unusually for Aberdaron, which rises up three steep hills from the centre, this cul de sac is on the flat. The cottage is modern and is simply appointed – no romantic old stone one-up, one-down. There is a garden that is crying out to be loved and cultivated and beyond the garden stretches an un-inhabited valley with no paths or access, only impenetrable scrub and bracken. Best of all, a stream runs the full length of house and garden. The ground rises steeply from the far bank of the stream so there is no long view from the sitting-room window. Thickets of gorse, blackthorn, hawthorn and ash saplings all but hide the few houses bordering the road at the top of the bank, many of which are second homes and lie empty all through the winter. So I would be amazingly secluded but also enfolded by the immediate natural surroundings. The move would be from the wide open spaces of the headland and Sound guarded by Bardsey, to the relative enclo-sure of a green 'cave', for the far bank of the stream is only a few yards from the windows. Both environs are actually 'traditional' settings for the eremitic life. The 'cave' excludes natural light and sensory stimuli both of beauty and of drabness, and sounds as well as sight are muted. For some this resonates with their inner land-scape. For me it is not so. My being expands in wide open spaces with long views. Yet these traditional equivalents are more figures of speech than actual realities in twenty-first-century Britain, but they remain meaningful metaphors. As I pondered the possibilities of this new hermitage/anchorhold, I could see that an eremitic life of prayer and imaginative seeking could certainly continue there in a new context and I could explore and learn to welcome this new gift. Some people are less conscious of their surroundings or perhaps expect less from life but that is not so for me. My being has become finely honed by what I see and the sounds around me that make up the actuality of a place for me. Now perhaps, the high green bank rising sharply only yards from the cottage windows will prove to be a metaphor in itself: a wall to be leapt over as these new surroundings shape the externals of my life. Either I resist change and fight against it, or I 'leap over the wall'.

For centuries, Aberdaron has been the end point for many pilgrims making their way along the two ancient pilgrim routes of the Llŷn Peninsula. The treacherous Sound frequently precludes any boat from setting out for Bardsey itself. The sea that washes up the beach within a few feet of Aberdaron church has guarded this ancient village for centuries, both welcoming and warning that the journey is one of *encounter*. Gradually the sea has encroached, threatening the survival of the small pilgrim church whose living stones have heard countless heart-deep prayers and echoed to the footfalls of thousands of feet. New sea defences keep the sea at bay at present but the coastline is eroding visibly year by year as the storms strengthen and become unpredictable and more frequent. The cliffs of compacted clay are sculpted into crenulations and fissures which change almost daily.

> . . . Now
> in the small hours
> of belief the one eloquence
>
> to master is that
> of the bowed head, the bent
> knee, waiting, as at the end
>
> of a hard winter
> for one flower to open
> on the mind's tree of thorns.[5]

---

5 Thomas, R. S., 2001, 'Waiting' in *Collected Poems 1945–1990*, Phoenix Press, p. 376.

The day of the move arrived, 2 January 2008. This would be rather different from the day of my arrival one spring 25 years ago when holding on for dear life I bowled over the fields in a small open sheep-transporter behind a tractor. Imagine moving home, however minimal the house contents, in mid-winter, across those same fields, now wet and muddy, down which it is impossible to get a removals van however small. Prior to Christmas I had filled dozens of black refuse bags, made several trips to the charity shops in Pwllheli and donated surplus books to the car park summer bookstall in Aberdaron. Even hermits collect clutter and I vowed to keep this at bay in the future. Whatever could be packed into boxes in advance was packed. Packing up made me realize how much I had 'needed', living as I did far from shops and utilities. I had had to be self-reliant in sorting out all sorts of breakdowns of appliances and house fabric let alone the garden and the diverse predators. It is amazing how Heath-Robinsonian remedies for many seemingly intractable problems could be made to last for weeks or even years. My friends used to tell me that cup-hooks and plastic-covered wire form a legacy wherever I have lived. My small cabin had expanded internally since my arrival with shelving over doorways and windows and extra storage space in every nook and cranny. In a 5 metre-square house, space is at a premium and clutter anathema. My new anchorage, though spacious indeed in comparison, was designed for short summer holiday lets only, so storage space was again at a premium. The cottage had a sitting room with a small kitchen at one end, a bedroom and bathroom with a shower, and a slip of a room that had been a bunkroom for children, the bunks – now removed – taking up all the space. At first, at least, I would need to use this slip of a room as a box room.

Earlier, at the end of 2007, the close friend with whom I had made that pilgrimage to Skellig Michael came up for a few days to help me in whatever way she could. Together we assembled flat-pack furniture amid a great deal of hilarity. There we were, two Cambridge graduates, standing on our heads trying to make out the diagrams and gobbledygook of the instructions – usually translated from

Swedish or Chinese – and taking four hours to finish an assembly that should have taken two. The wardrobe was almost our Waterloo with its three doors, three shelves, three drawers and hanging compartment. The doors needed to close and to stay closed. I brought in trustworthy help. However we were well pleased with the final results of our efforts. All was now as ready as it could be in advance of the move itself.

I listened to the weather and shipping forecasts for early January with minute attention and prayed for a window between the storms. We had a tight schedule, as another friend, who was very familiar with the area having been here for her retreats for many years, planned to come up with a large four-wheel drive estate car that could manage virtually any terrain but she only had a few days free. Two other local friends each with small four-wheel drive trucks of doubtful negotiability on muddy slopes had also offered their help. Kind Wil from the farm, having shaken his head consistently at the stupidity of my plan to move in January, said he could be on hand with his tractor and trailer in the afternoon of the proposed D-Day should all else fail. My heart sank at the thought of carrying furniture, especially bed and mattress, through the garden and out into the field in pouring rain. As far as possible contingency plans were in place.

The day dawned cloudy but dry and still, and the fields were reasonably negotiable. Friend and large estate car came bright and early and we started loading up. Out of the corner of my eye I saw one of the other vehicles – the little yellow truck – bouncing across the field with its strong male driver at the wheel. The next thing we knew it was stuck in the mud outside my gate. After much laying down of sacking, use of strategic rocks and sheer hands-on pushing, the truck was rescued and we revived ourselves with mugs of extra-strong coffee. I don't think I had laughed so much for many a long day. Eventually all was loaded. I was coming back the following day to clean up and say my goodbyes to the farm so this was not the final leave-taking. That came later as I locked the door for the last time and roped the gate. Admittedly rather full up I was also full of thanksgiving and, with that unique view etched indelibly on my mind's eye, I felt ready to move forward tentatively.

Halfway down to Aberdaron in the little yellow truck, my driver's mobile rang persistently. Answering it, anxiety filled the car. He was urgently needed as our other removals friend due to meet us in the village had been taken ill and needed immediate help. Here we were with the truck full of my furniture and neither still in Tŷ Pren nor yet in Aberdaron. We hardly knew whether to laugh or to cry, both equally inappropriate. So we continued down to Aberdaron where help with unloading was soon mobilized and the little yellow truck sped off all lights flashing. Both for my friends and for the move the story ended well. The furniture was soon in place and with time on our hands to our great surprise, we went back to Tŷ Pren, cleaned right through and I said my goodbyes as best I could, for sadness was closely mingled with anticipation.

The actual move was accomplished and I sank thankfully into bed that night, alert to new sounds in the silence and lulled to sleep by the whispering of the stream running past my window and the faint roar of the sea as the waves broke against the cliffs in Aberdaron bay. How different it all seemed.

I have not moved far from the *place* which gave my solitary journey life and form. Yet though I am now only three miles from that square mile at the tip of the Peninsula opposite Bardsey it is a move from a marked degree of remoteness to one among people, however minimally. It felt like a move of many miles. The district of Uwchmynydd, which borders the far headlands of Pen Llŷn, remains relatively untouched by the recent fast-moving changes affecting most of the rest of western society. The old way of life and customs of the more remote parts of rural Llŷn have not really moved into the present day though TV, mechanization and greater mobility are bringing change. Aberdaron, only three miles away, with its flow of tourists and 'pilgrims' and many incomers, is to my surprise a *markedly* different place. It will take time for me to 'inhabit' these new surroundings, to lean into the given and welcome it.

One chapter of my life begins to move into the next and I sense myself to be at a bridging time. Bridging had always been an element of my eremitic life but this now was of a different quality. Just as trees now meet my gaze as I pray and a mere two-minute walk takes me to Aberdaron bay where the rollers of the open sea sweep toward the land patterning the sands, so at my heart's centre the tides ebb and flow.

Now, as I write, I look back over my first six months here with mixed feelings but an unwavering underlying sense of thankfulness and expectancy. Yesterday I went over to Bardsey for the day to take stock on the Island where I know I can breathe freely and am integrated in a way that I cannot expect to feel as yet in my new anchorhold. Bardsey was central to and on the edge of the *place* I had inhabited for so long. Aberdaron also borders that place but has little sense of being radically on the edge. As I sat on the rocks of Bardsey's western seaboard, I gazed out at the vastness of the unbroken horizon. Once more I was given a sense of perspective and proportion to guide me through the next months or however long the effects of the move take to find a new level. I recently transplanted a sapling from the pot where it had been nurtured and sheltered from a seed to early maturity. As I teased out the roots of the matted root ball and planted it in the carefully prepared and manured new planting hole, I knew it would take time for the roots to penetrate the soil and new rootlets to grow. There are no short cuts and only rarely is it right to use the surgeon's scalpel to cut off a limb ruthlessly or to pluck out an offending eye. My temperament would prefer the surgeon's knife but this is unrealistic and an evasion of the real issues. From my new anchorage, if I climb one of the steep hills out of Aberdaron, I can reach the cliff path overlooking the bay and over the wider waters of Cardigan Bay itself before the cliffs round the point where the mainland borders the Sound and looks over to Bardsey. This will surely become a favourite prayer place and rock there above the bay. When August fills Aberdaron to bursting point and there are no places empty of the influx, maybe I shall realize that my own garden and the bank of the stream are now where my prayer-rock is to be.

To the one who knows nothing, mountains are mountains, waters are waters and trees are trees. But when he has studied and knows a little, mountains are no longer mountains, water is no longer water, and trees are no longer trees. But when he has thoroughly understood, mountains are once again mountains, waters are waters and trees are trees. (Zen Buddhist saying)

Epilogue

Three journeys have been woven together in the pages of this narrative, 'three stories: the story of a place, a personal journey lived out within that place, and the universal journey shared by all men and women – our human condition' – of which each personal journey is a part.

As we have seen the earliest historical traces and records of monasticism in *this place* make it almost certain that the monks came as missionaries with probably little knowledge of their destination beyond the fact that no Christians had been here before them. They did not come primarily to draw apart in order to pray except in the sense that worship and prayer were an integral part of the basic rhythm of their lives, but they came to establish a small monastic settlement from which they could evangelize their immediate surroundings. They did not arrive overland through the rough terrain of scrub and rock with few well-worn tracks or anything that would have passed as a road. They came by sea. The inshore waters were an open highway and this coast may well have been part of a trade route up the west side of Britain northward to Scotland and westward over to Ireland. Many years passed before a few of these early monks began to seek a less activist lifestyle for a more contemplative life. At first they found more remote places locally such as Anelog in Uwchmynydd; only later did they venture across the treacherous Sound to Bardsey. At first they may have visited the Island for periods of greater austerity such as Lent. Only gradually did a very few withdraw alone to live as hermits.

The land lent itself to their quest. It was rugged and inhospitable, difficult to cultivate, exposed to the extremes of the elemental storms: a veritable desert in the monastic tradition on which their lives were based. So the land itself became a part of the quest: a quest for holiness as this was understood in the early Middle Ages, yet coloured by the indigenous culture of this Celtic fringe of northwest Wales. Holiness draws holiness. Islands in particular have a certain mystique, with their natural boundaries of sea and storm, and draw those questing to themselves. So Bardsey began to be known as a 'holy island'; its very geography enhanced its image, with a mountain whose summit appeared closer to the heavens than the coastal mainland and whose surrounding treacherous seas claimed many 'martyrs' into their depths. This was still an age when the world was believed to be flat and three-tiered and the Island was a living metaphor. (As we have seen Skellig Michael is an even more vivid example of an offshore island whose peak seemed to reach up to the heavens and whose rocks rose out of the turbulent darkness of the untameable oceans and underworld.) Each evening the day died as the sun sank below the western horizon. Each morning it rose again to new life with the dawn from the east. Gradually the understanding of what radiated holiness changed. The culture of each succeeding age shaped the quest and the quest influenced the culture while this was still an age in which faith and belief were the norm. The quest here in Pen Llŷn, in *this place*, continued throughout this medieval time and beyond with few significant breaks. Something integral to this place drew seekers to itself, and hermits.

Holy lives leave an imprint on the land where they have been lived. There are many levels in which to interpret this: through imagery, poetry, music, storytelling and above all, silence and solitude. Here on Pen Llŷn this imprint, this sense of those who have gone before, is almost tangible, can be sensed in ways beyond the everyday literal reach of our five senses. The veil between time and eternity, between life and death is gossamer thin, as it is in sleep or the inner caverns of the heart in prayer. Boundaries are crossed between land and sea as the tides wash in and out, as the sands lie patterned after the sea recedes and the abandoned sea anemones cling to the rocks until the tide washes in once more. Circling high above the ocean's depth the gannet dives with an accuracy that defies sight as we know it. Here the adage that 'the ear translates, it does not hear; the eye reproduces, it does not see', is certainly a reality as an awakening attentiveness grows from within, 'deep calling to deep'. Life coming towards us is welcomed for what it may unveil. There is a heightened sense of expectancy mellowing into hope. Concepts and even interpretations have no place if they freeze what is continually in movement and put it into a box that can be labelled and understood in purely logical/rational terms seemingly under our control. The creativity of the living Spirit has no bounds other than itself. In the present moment, the past lives on and the future lies wide open.

Our masks do not fool God but neither are they removed until the time is right and we begin to see them for ourselves. There is a great deal of painful discovery on this journey where God is the centre and the context. This is an ambience that was natural to the early Middle Ages and was seen as one in which the seeming opposites of life could be transcended and transformation and reconciliation could begin. In our psychologically orientated culture where many think we hold the dominion, are in control, this is a view that finds little credence. Yet in a life that is attuned to the sense that we are not *ultimately* in control this transformation does begin and we are gradually brought home to ourselves. Home to ourselves and therefore to God, for God is both the initiator and the response – a theme that has recurred throughout this narrative. But this is not confined only to those who profess a faith in God, but also to some who seek from different outlooks on life but nevertheless find themselves on this same journey interpreted by them in other ways. Maybe it is we who ring-fence the workings of the Spirit. It seems that in this *place*, Pen Llŷn, all down the ages, men and women have found an environment which is conducive to their quest and to solitude – if solitude is the way for them – yet

not for themselves alone but as part of the life of the whole world.
The whole of the universe is interconnected, and awareness of this
grows as the quest deepens.

> It might be their own white strength
> that keeps the faith-flame steady
> in the solitary sisters, one
> living a slow dance
> inland in the valley with her bees,
> the other at the edge, perched
> where fields fall away to greyness,
> to the set or fret of the sea.
> All day in all seasons she faces out,
> attentive to the spring-returning dolphins,
> missing the white hare's brightness in the dead bracken.
> Sees how the heather when it blows
> shrinks back, survives the burning.
>
> All night swept by the loom
> of the unseen lighthouse, opening wings,
> she feels the small white wooden cabin,
> her anchor-hold, tilting to each
> shove of the wind, each salt lash
> of rain. It must feel like moving
> forward, urged out of the dark;
> towards landfall on a looked-for shore.
>
> In mid-winter, as we cross the Sound
> back from delivering the island Christmas mail,
> sunset flaring in her window
> makes for us a better Advent candle,
> than buds of light on a dead tree.[1]

---

1 Evans, Christine, 2006, *Burning the Candle*, Gomer Press, p. 33.

No solitary would attribute to herself this impact of her life that the poem expresses, this impact of her life on the edge, on the cliff top of a headland in this *place*. The author feels that she has no faith she can claim as her own – perhaps no set of beliefs or anyone she could name as God, but faith. Yet perhaps there is a radiant reflection here of what I myself had gradually become aware as an imprint on the land itself of those who had had gone before. At times, when my faith seems particularly shrouded in mists and all manner of doubts invade the heart and mind, the awareness of the legacy of those whose quest was lived out here down the ages and the seeming recognition that a similar quest is still drawing others here now, fills me with hope. Often their quest is not in the name of any 'god' that they could claim except in the sense that there is something more to life than linear time and the material world. And perhaps hope is the key to all these lives expressed in such different ways from within the cultures of each age, the key to all three stories.

> There is a geography of holy places, the places where the saints have dwelt. . . . Places whose beauty has been revealed by lives which have been open to God in such a way as to show that this world is not a system closed upon itself. These are places whose power persists through centuries of indifference and neglect to be revealed again when men are ready for it. Places which display the potential holiness of all this earth which man has loved so much yet so much ravaged.[2]

Questing, seeking, has its roots in hope: hope that the quest is not just for oneself but is intrinsic also to the ongoing life of the whole world and somehow helping to bring about change for good in however small a way. This openness touches all our lives whatever our circumstances if we give it houseroom. The aloneness and the

---

2 Allchin, A. M., 1978, *The World is a Wedding*, Darton, Longman and Todd, p. 20.

listening attentiveness that is so central to the hermit can find expression in every life and could perhaps help some to find doorways out of loneliness and others to deepen their great concern for the poor and destitute and suffering, let alone the sense that we are destroying the very earth on which we live.

Listening and attentiveness go hand in hand with prayer and worship. Yet what are prayer and worship? God does not need our praise, our tribute. God is all in all: 'I AM' – that is God's name. Prayer does not 'change *God's* mind', but it alters *us, our* perceptions. This is within the reach of all of us however busy our life. Through prayer, through attentiveness and stillness at our heart's centre, *we* are gradually transformed and begin to discern the way forward, the path to tread. And this 'transformation' is contagious; it ripples out in ways of which we are unaware. We respond where we see compassion and love in others. Love stands at the intersection of our inhumanity to one another and our ravaging of the earth, and begins to transform it.

In Jacob's struggle at the ford of Jabbok (Gen. 32.24–32), after wrestling all night with his 'unknown' adversary, Jacob cries out, 'I will not let you go unless you bless me.' He came away from the encounter with a new name but also wounded, limping, and overawed for, 'I have seen God face to face, and yet my life is preserved'. Perhaps this goes to the heart of the solitary's quest. So many, particularly in our present day and age, have struggled to maintain or find a faith in God in the face of almost unbelievable atrocities perpetrated by humankind, let alone the 'natural' disasters that we cannot avert. They have struggled but found no way through. In the play, *The Last days of Judas Iscariot* by Stephen Adly Guirgis, one of the characters says, 'Between heaven and hell, there is another place. This place is called hope.' The solitary continues to wrestle and the struggle 'for a blessing' is persistent as part of, and for, the whole world.

For me personally that has been the crossing point of Mother Mary Clare's saying:

A person who prays, maybe someone committed to the life of a hermit, can learn to live at the point of intersection where the Love of God and the tensions and suffering we inflict on one another, meet, and are held to God's transforming Love.

This for me has become a place of hope. Hope is born and reborn through doubt and questioning and times both of despondency and blessing, through disappointments and wrong turnings taken, and through times of peace and beauty. God is both the call and the response, the one who transforms. And this is the human journey we all share personally and corporately whether we can name God or not, for God lives within each one of us and in our relationships with one another, whether recognized or not.

> I thank you, deep power
> that works me ever more lightly
> in ways I cannot make out.
> The day's labour grows simpler now,
> and like a holy face
> held in my dark hands.[3]

---

3 Rilke, R. M., 1996, 'Thanksgiving: So bin ich nur als Kind erwacht', in *Rilke's Book of Hours: Love Poems to God*, trans. Anita Barrows and Joana Macey, Riverhead Books, p. 147.

Selected Reading

Abhishiktananda, 1998, *Ascent to the Depths of the Heart*, ed. R. Panikkar, trans. D. Fleming and J. Stuart, ISPCK

Allchin, A. M. (ed.), 1977, *Solitude and Communion: Papers on the Hermit Life*, SLG Press

Allchin, A. M., 1991, *Praise Above All: Discovering the Welsh tradition*, University of Wales Press

Armstrong, K., 1993, *A History of God: The 4000-year Quest of Judaism, Christianity and Islam*, Heinemann

Athanasius, 1980, *The Life of Antony and the Letter to Marcellinus*, trans. R. C. Gregg, Classics of Western Spirituality, SPCK

Beausobre, J. de, 1945, *Flame in the Snow: A Russian Legend*, Constable

Borg, M., 2003, *The Heart of Christianity: Rediscovering a Life of Faith*, HarperOne

Burton-Christie, D., 1993, *The Word in the Desert: Scripture and the Quest for Holiness in Early Christian Monasticism*, Oxford University Press

Chitty, M., 1992 and 2002, *The Monks on Ynys Enlli, Pts 1 & 2*, published privately

Clément, O., 1993, *The Roots of Christian Mysticism*, New City

Dalrymple, W., 1998, *From the Holy Mountain*, Flamingo

Davies, O. and Bowie, F. (eds), 1995, *Celtic Christian Spirituality: An Anthology of Medieval and Modern Sources*, SPCK

Davies, O., 1996, *Celtic Spirituality in Early Medieval Wales*, University of Wales Press

Davies, O. with O'Loughlin, T. (eds and trans.), 1999, *Celtic Spirituality*, Paulist Press

Dillard, A., 1988, *Pilgrim at Tinker Creek*, Harper Perennial Modern Classics

Finch, R. M. (trans.), 1986, *The Way of the Pilgrim*, Triangle, SPCK

Hammarskjöld, D., 1994, *Markings*, trans. L. Sjöberg and W. H. Auden, Ballantine Books.

Harvey, A., 1983, *A Journey in Ladakh*, Jonathan Cape

Hughes, G. W. SJ, 1997, *God, Where Are You?*, Darton, Longman and Todd

Jamison, C. OSB, 2006, *Finding Sanctuary: Monastic Steps for Everyday Life*, Weidenfeld & Nicolson

Jung, C., 1971, *Memories, Dreams, Reflections*, Fontana

Laird, M., 2006, *Into the Silent Land: The Practice of Contemplation*, Darton, Longman and Todd

Lane, B., 1998, *The Solace of Fierce Landscapes: Exploring Mountain and Desert Spirituality*, Oxford University Press

Louth, A., 1991, *The Wilderness of God*, Darton, Longman and Todd

Matthews, I. OCD, 1995, *The Impact of God: Soundings from St John of the Cross*, Hodder & Stoughton

Matthews, M., 2000, *Both Alike to Thee: The Retrieval of the Mystical Way*, SPCK

Mayne, M., 1995, *This Sunrise of Wonder: Letters for the Journey*, Fount

Mott, M., 1984, *The Seven Mountains of Thomas Merton*, Sheldon Press, SPCK

Nicholl, D., 1998, *The Testing of Hearts: A Pilgrim's Journey*, Darton, Longman and Todd.

O'Donohue, J., 1999, *Anam Cara: Spiritual Wisdom of the Celtic World*, Bantam

Radcliffe, T. OP, 2005, *What Is the Point of Being a Christian?*, Continuum

Rilke, R. M., 1996, *Rilke's Book of Hours: Love Poems to God*, trans. A. Barrow and J. Macy, Riverhead Books

Sheldrake, P., 1996, *Living Between Worlds: Place and Journey in Celtic Spirituality*, Darton, Longman and Todd

Smith, C. OSB, 1987, *The Way of Paradox: Spiritual Life as Taught by Meister Eckhart*, Darton, Longman and Todd

Sogyal Rimpoche, 1992, *The Tibetan Book of Living and Dying*, ed. P. Caffney and A. Harvey, Rider.

Ward, B. SLG, 1975, *The Sayings of the Desert Fathers*, Mowbray

Ward, B. (introd.) and Russell, N. (trans.), 1981, *The Lives of the Desert Fathers*, Mowbray

Williams, R., 2000, *Reflections on Cultural Bereavement*, Continuum

Williams, R., 2000, *Christ on Trial: How the Gospels Unsettle Our Judgement*, Fount

Williams, R., 2002, *Writing in the Dust: Reflections on 11th September and its Aftermath*, Hodder & Stoughton

Williams, R., 2003, *Silence and Honeycakes*, Lion

Selected Poets

Auden, W. H., 1968, *Selected Poems*, Faber and Faber

Bowen, Euros. Davies, C. and S. (eds), 1993, *Euros Bowen: Priest-Poet*, Church in Wales Publications

Coleridge, S. T., 2008, *The Rime of the Ancient Mariner*, Enitharmon Press

Donne, John, 2004, *The Complete English Poems*, ed. A. J. Smith, Penguin Classics

Evans, Christine, 1989, *Cometary Phases*, Seren Books, Poetry Wales Press Ltd; 2006, *Burning the Candle*, Gomer Press

Eliot, T. S., 2004, *The Complete Poems and Plays*, Faber and Faber

Frost, Robert, 1943, *Collected Poems*, Jonathan Cape

Herbert, George, 2004, *The Complete English Poems*, ed. John Tobin, Penguin Classics

Hopkins, G. M., 1948, *Poems*, 3rd edn, Oxford University Press

O'Siadhal, Michael, 2002, *The Gossamer Walk: Poems in Witness to the Holocaust*, Bloodaxe Books

Rumi, 2004, *Selected Poems*, trans. Coleman Barks, Penguin Classics

Ryōkan. See M. L. Kownacki, 2004, *Between Two Souls: Conversations with Ryōkan*, Eerdmans

Scott, David, 2005 *Piecing Together*, Bloodaxe Books

Thomas, R. S., 2001, *Collected Poems 1945–1990*, Phoenix Press

Traherne, Thomas, 1966, *Poems, Centuries and Three Thanksgivings*, ed. Anne Ridler, Oxford University Press

Vaughan, Henry, 2004, *Selected Poems*, ed. Anne Cluysenaar, SPCK

Williams, Waldo, 1997, *The Peacemakers*, trans. Tony Conran, Gomer Press

Yeats, W. B., 1991, *Collected Poems*, Macmillan

Acknowledgements of Sources

The authors and publisher gratefully acknowledge permission to use the following material under copyright:

W. H. Auden, 'In Memory of W. B. Yeats', in *Selected Poems*, Faber & Faber and Random House, 1968 edition, p. 42.

Christine Evans, 'The Beauty of the Taper', in *Burning the Candle*, Gomer Press, 2006.

Robert Frost, 'Stopping by the Woods on a Snowy Evening', in *Collected Poems of Robert Frost*, Jonathan Cape, 1943 edition, p. 275. Permission requested.

Mary Lou Kownaki, *Between Two Souls: Conversations with Ryōkan*, Eerdman's, 2004. From the translated texts in © John Stevens (translator), *Dewdrops on a Lotus Leaf: Zen Poems by Ryōkan*, Shambhala Publications, 1993. Permission requested.

Morgan Llwyd, 'Contemplation' and 'A Treasury of Welsh Spirituality', in Brian Brendan O'Malley, editor (trans. Cynthia Saunders Davies), *A Welsh Pilgrim's Manual/Cydymaith y Pererinion*, Gomer Press, 1989.

Michael O'Siadhail, 'Repair', in *The Gossamer Wall*, Bloodaxe Books, 2002, p. 121.

Rainer Maria Rilke, 'Thanksgiving: So bin ich nur als Kind erwacht', from *Rilke's Book of Hours: Love Poems to God*, translated by Anita Barrows and Joana Macey, copyright © 1996 by Anita Barrows and Joanna Macey. Used by permission of Riverhead Books, an imprint of Penguin Group (USA) Inc.

Cynthia Saunders Davies, editor, *Euros Bowen, Priest-Poet, Metamorphosis*, Church in Wales Publications, 1993, p. 29.

David Scott, 'Skellig Michael', in *Selected Poems*, Bloodaxe Books, 1997.

R. S. Thomas, 'The Other', 'Fugue to Ann Griffiths', 'Moorland', 'Sea-Watching', 'Pilgrimages', 'Waiting' and 'The Moon in Lleyn', in *Collected Poems 1945–1990*, Phoenix Press, 2001.

Waldo Williams, 'Tŷ Ddewi' (trans. Dafydd Johnston), in Waldo Williams (trans. Tony Conran), *The Peacemakers*, Gomer Press, 1997.